Turkey in Europe

Turkey in Europe:
benefit or catastrophe?

Roberto de Mattei

Translated by John Laughland

GRACEWING

First published in Italian as *La Turchia in Europa*
by SugarCo Edizioni, 2009

First published in English, 2009

Gracewing
2 Southern Avenue, Leominster
Herefordshire, HR6 0QF

The right of Roberto de Mattei to be identified as the author of this work has been asserted in accordance with the Copyright, Designs and Patents Act 1988.

ISBN 978 0 85244 732 1

Typset by Action Publishing Technology Ltd, Gloucester GL1 5SR

Contents

Chapter One

Turkey in History

A large country seeking to enter Europe

The institutions and governments of Europe are currently involved in a complex negotiation over Turkey's accession to the European Union. The Republic of Turkey (*Türkiye Cumhuriyeti*) is a large country situated in a strategic part of the world. Its geopolitical position, its demographic weight, its economic potential, and also the beauty of its landscape and the hospitality of its inhabitants, make it a possible partner and certainly not an enemy of Europe. However, the relationship involved in a partnership is different from full membership of the EU institutions. Many doubts and questions have been raised in recent years on this subject. The problem discussed in this study can be expressed as follows: would the accession of Turkey to the EU constitute a benefit or an irreparable catastrophe for our continent? This is a question which needs to be examined deeply and without prejudice since it has a direct impact on our future and on that of our children.

An Asian peninsula with a European appendage

On the map, Turkey appears as an Asian peninsula surrounded by the Black Sea to the north, the Mediterranean to the south and the Aegean to the west. Its territory, which comprises 780,066 square kilometres, is composed almost entirely of Anatolia (755,688 km²) with just a small European part, Eastern Thrace (24,378 km²). The Bosphorus and the Dardanelles, the straits at either end of the Sea of Marmara, separate the vastness of Asian Turkey from her small European part which constitutes but one thirtieth of the total territory.

Asian Turkey borders Syria, Iraq, Iran, Georgia, Armenia and Azerbaijan; European Turkey borders Bulgaria and Greece. From the geopolitical point of view, Turkey belongs to the regional sub-system of the Middle East. Historically, Anatolia was the cradle of a multitude of civilisations and peoples who settled there. These include the Hittites, the Phrygians, the Thracians, the Lydians, the Armenians and the Greeks. Incorporated into the Persian, Macedonian, Roman and Byzantine empires, Anatolia was, for many centuries, in the Greco-Roman and later Christian sphere of influence,[1] when it was known as Asia Minor. However, over the centuries the human geography of the region changed profoundly. Turkish Islam came to dominate the area and the border of the Ottoman Empire constituted the south-eastern limit of Europe and of its history.[2]

From the region of Altai to the gates of Vienna

The Turks of today are the descendants of nomadic tribes who migrated from the Asian steppe in the sixth century, especially from the remote region of Altai.[3] Anatolia was where these peoples settled and, over time, they superimposed themselves on other ethnic groups – Mongolian, Iranian, Caucasian and Indo-European. From the eighth century onwards, what bound them together and gave them the strength to project themselves outwards, was the Muslim religion. For Islam, the Turks were in the East what the Arabs were in the West – peoples who conquered in the name of Allah and his prophet.

[1]. Freely, 2006.
[2]. Halecki, 1962, p. 83.
[3]. Pitcher, 1972, pp. 22–3.

In 732, a century after the death of Mohammed, Arab expansionism in the West was stopped at Poitiers by the French army under Charles Martel. In the East, between the tenth and thirteenth centuries, the Seljuk dynasty ruled over the territory of today's Turkey, later extending its dominion to Persia, Syria and Iraq and consolidating the Sunni-Muslim faith. From the thirteenth century onwards, the Seljuks were succeeded by the Ottomans (the dynasty took its name from the Sultan Osman) who united under their rule large parts of the Byzantine empire and the Arab world.[4]

The Crusades delivered a setback to Muslim expansion but in the fourteenth century it again embarked on conquest. After having defeated the Christian resistance at the Battle of Kosovo Field in 1389, at Nicopolis in 1396 and at Varna in 1444, the Turkish armies, under Sultan Mohammed II, conquered Constantinople in 1453. The former capital of the Eastern Roman empire changed its name to Istanbul and became the new capital of the Ottoman Empire. From then on, the threatening shadow of the Turks followed European history like a nightmare. The claim made by the historian Jason Goodwin that the Ottoman empire 'lived by war' is not wrong.[5] From its foundation to its collapse, the Ottoman Empire was a state dedicated to expanding the Islamic faith by force of arms.[6]

The voices of the Roman Pontiffs were often raised in defence of Christendom, promoting 'Holy Leagues' against the Turks as did Pius V in 1571 and Blessed Innocent XI in 1683. The Venetian Republic, with its diplomacy and armed forces, was on the front line against the Ottomans in a 'widened' Mediterranean which stretched to the coasts of the Black Sea.

The Ottoman Sultans, who assumed the title of caliph from 1517 onwards, subjugated the Orthodox Balkans and

---

[4] On the Ottoman Empire, see Bombaci and Shaw, 1981; Mantran, 1989; Kinross, 2002; McCarthy, 2005; Goffman, 2007; Quataert, 2007; Faroqhi, 2008.
[5] Goodwin, Jason, 1998, p. 65.
[6] Lewis, *The Emergence of Modern Turkey*, p. 13.

reached Belgrade. They conquered Hungary in 1526 and reached the gates of Vienna twice, first in 1529 and then again in 1683. 'For nearly a thousand years,' the historian Bernard Lewis reminds us, 'from the day when the Moors first landed in Spain to the second Turkish siege of Vienna, Europe lived under the constant threat of Islam.'[7]

Between the sixteenth and seventeenth centuries, the Ottoman Empire covered a territory of some 6,000,000 km^2, extending from Algeria to Arabia into the Middle East beyond Baghdad and including the Crimea, Bulgaria, Romania, Hungary and the Balkans.

This expansion was finally stopped by the Christian fleet at the Battle of Lepanto in 1571 and then at Vienna by the Imperial army led by the King of Poland, John Sobieski, in 1683. The Ottoman declaration of war delivered to the Habsburg Emperor, Leopold I, said, 'We are going to hit your little country by war and trample it to the ground . . . We order you to wait for us at Vienna so that we can decapitate you, you infamous one among the creatures of God, as one does only with an infidel.'[8]

The rout of the Turks at the gates of Vienna was followed by a series of defeats and the losses of cities and provinces. Budapest was liberated in 1686, Belgrade in 1717. The Austrian Empire imposed on the Turks the humiliating Treaties of Carlowitz in 1699 and Passerowitz in 1718 which marked the decline of Ottoman power.

Decline and fall of the Ottoman Empire

The final decline of the Ottoman Empire was sealed by the Russian-Turkish war of 1768–76. The treaty of Kücük Kanyarka which concluded the war signalled the beginning of the 'Eastern question' in which the Western powers were divided over the destiny of the Ottoman Empire.

Whereas in the seventeenth and eighteenth centuries, the

7. Lewis, 1995, p. 26.
8. Stürminger, 1983, p. 27; Ricci, 2008, p. 41.

principal enemy of Turkey was the Austrian Empire, in the nineteenth century it became the Russian Empire, which
contested the Ottomans' supremacy over the Caucasian
regions of the Black Sea. In the first decades of the nineteenth
century, the first two Balkan uprisings against Ottoman power
occurred: in Serbia in 1804 and in Greece in 1821. The
Crimean War (1853–56) marked a fundamental change and
the 'Sublime Porte' – as the Ottoman Empire was then
referred to – became part of the 'Concert of Europe' by
allying itself with France, Great Britain and the Kingdom of
Sardinia against Russia. Under pressure from its new allies, the
Ottoman Sultans undertook a series of 'Europeanising' reforms
which ensured greater liberties for their Christian subjects.

Sultan Abdul Mejid I (1839–1861) who had proclaimed the
inviolability of life and property in an edict (*Hatt-i-Sharif*) in
1839, guaranteed freedom of religion for his citizens with a
second edict in 1856. These 'reforms' (*tanzimat*) culminated
in the first constitution in the Muslim world. However it had little
effect and provoked strong counter-reactions. The reign of
Abdul Hamid II (1876–1909), the last Ottoman autocrat, was
characterised by despotism and by the attempt to re-launch
a pan-Islamic policy. At the same time, and with the help of
European Freemasonry, the Party of the Young Turks started to
assert itself, a revolutionary movement composed mainly of
young officials who fought for the secularisation of the
country and who won power in 1908.[9]

The First World War (1914–18), preceded by the Balkan
conflict of 1912–13, found the Ottoman Empire on the side
of Germany and Austria against the powers of the 'Triple
Entente' (Russia, France and Great Britain). The Empire
suffered serious defeats and was forced to surrender in the
autumn of 1918. French forces settled temporarily in Cilicia,
Italians between Ankara and the Mediterranean coast, the
British on the Black Sea, while the Greek army occupied
Eastern Thrace and Istanbul. The Treaty of Sèvres of 10
August 1920 sanctioned the complete dismemberment of

9. Lewis, *The Emergence of Modern Turkey*, pp. 210–38.

the Empire and seemed to signal the end of this Islamic power.[10]

The 'cultural revolution' of Kemal Atatürk

It was at this point that a man entered the scene who was destined to become the hero of modern Turkey: General Mustafa Kemal (1881–1938), an officer from Salonica who had belonged to the 'Young Turks' and who had fought with distinction at the Dardanelles in the First World War.

Between 1919 and 1923, the Turkish army, led by Kemal, rebelled against the defeatist government in Istanbul and, starting from Anatolia, succeeded in conquering the peninsula. After winning the Straits and Thrace, Kemal obtained recognition of his full sovereignty over the whole of Turkish territory, which prevented it being divided up between the Allies.

On 24 July 1923, the conference of Lausanne redefined Turkey as a nation state while the Arab regions which had been part of the former Ottoman empire were put under European 'mandate' until such time as they would achieve full political autonomy.

On 29 October 1923 Mustafa Kemal became the first president of the Turkish Republic which was created in a break with the Ottoman tradition. The abolition of the Sultanate on 1 November 1922 and of the Caliphate on 3 March 1924 marked a historic change which was sealed by moving the capital from Constantinople to Ankara.

After taking power, Mustafa Kemal led his own genuine 'cultural revolution' in the name of 'modernisation' which was to become known as 'Kemalism'.[11] The fundamental principles of Kemalism – defined as 'six arrows' – were: populism, which rejected any class-based vision of society in the name of 'the people'; republicanism, which broke the link with the Ottoman monarchy; nationalism, which affirmed the ethnopolitical primacy of 'Turkishness'; secularism, which brought

[10.] Fromkin, 2002.
[11.] Cf. Lewis, *The Emergence of Modern Turkey*; Mango, 2004; Zürcher, 2007.

religion back under the control of the state; statism, which stood for the economic doctrines in vogue in the 1930s; and reformism, which represented the will to effect a revolutionary change in Ottoman society.

With these reforms implemented in the 1920s and 1930s, Mustafa Kemal tried to dissociate the Turkish people once and for all from its Ottoman past in order to create a new 'modern' national identity. The American philosopher John Dewey (1859–1952) was the first in a series of Western scholars to be invited by the Turkish government to help elaborate the new national education policy to promote the secularisation and Westernisation of the country.[12]

Kemal, to whom the name Atatürk ('father of the Turks') was given, died on 10 November 1938. His ideology survived under the leadership of his right-hand man, Ismet Inönü (1884–1973), president of the Turkish Republic until 1950, who had to face the tensions coming from the Muslim world which opposed the secularisation of the state.

After changing its position during the Second World War, moving from neutrality to alignment with the Allies in 1944, Turkey entered the system of Western alliances. In 1951 the country joined NATO and anti-Soviet missiles and bases were installed on its territory. The Western governments, a British historian has written, 'did not only supply the country with huge amounts of financial aid; they also looked benevolently and uncritically at its unstable dictatorial regimes – often the result of military coups – and its grave violations of the rights of minorities'.[13] In this period, tens of thousands of Turkish workers emigrated *en masse* to other European countries in search of employment.

Although different political parties were established from the 1950s onwards, the country did not become a true democracy. The Turkish army assumed the role of the 'guarantor' of Kemalism and intervened repeatedly in politics, in 1960, 1971, 1980 and 1997, to restore secular 'orthodoxy'

[12.] Caligiuri, 2007.
[13.] Judt, 2007, p. 946.

against attempts to re-Islamise the country. A Prime Minister, Adnan Menderes (1899–1961), was hanged in 1961 after having been accused of wanting to restore Islam to public life.

Of the eleven heads of state between 1924 and today, six have been senior army officers. They lost power for the first time in 2002 when the (Islamic) Justice and Development Party (*Adalet ve Kalkinma Partisi* or AKP) led by Recep Tayyip Erdogan, won the elections in 2002, a victory repeated in the elections of July 2007. Since 2002, therefore, Turkey has been governed by an Islamist party which controls the national parliament with a two-thirds majority and which can therefore govern as if there were a one-party system. The political scientist, Alexandre del Valle, has defined 3 November 2002, the day when Erdogan was elected, as the date of the 'second death', both symbolic and electoral, of Atatürk.[14]

A country with multiple identities . . .

Today Turkey is a country with 72,000,000 inhabitants of which ethnic Turks make up some 86%. The dominant religion is Islam (98%). But in spite of this apparent homogeneity, Turkey is a country with a complex history in which multiple identities overlie one another.

According to the sociologist Massimo Introvigne,[15] Turkey has at least four different identities. The first and the strongest remains its Muslim identity. This is expressed by that politico-spiritual community, the *Umma*, which for a while was led by the Prophet and by the first Caliphs. The rest of the world is considered to be 'the house of war' (*dār-al-harb*) which needs to be conquered. This pan-Islamic identity finds its symbolic expression in the annual commemoration of the conquest of Constantinople in 1453 and in nostalgia for the former primacy of the Empire, which was the seat of the Caliphate until it was suppressed in 1924. In Anatolia, that is

---

[14.] Del Valle, 2004, p. 88. See also Kaylam, 2005, pp. 409–27.
[15.] Introvigne, 2006, pp. 7–18.

in the major part of the country, a rural or semi-rural population, above all Sunni Muslim, which has endogamous and
archaic customs and a very high birth rate, lives principally
under the influence of this Islamic and Asian identity.

The second identity is that of the Ottoman Empire, above
all in its last phases, when it constituted a sort of 'confederation' which was multinational and religiously tolerant. This
Empire, which extended to Arabia, the Balkans and Libya,
included hundreds of ethnic groups and scores of religions
which were subordinated to the dominant religion of Islam.
Among these, some were recognised as *millet*, ethno-
religious communities to which a special status was applied:
Greek Orthodox, Jewish and Armenian but not Catholic.

The third identity is Turkish national identity, which appeared
for the first time in the middle of the nineteenth century in
small intellectual circles and which developed, thanks to
Atatürk, in the first half of the twentieth century. Within Turkish
nationalism there flow together pan-Turkism and the
'Turanism' of the Young Turks,[16] based on the conviction that
all peoples who speak Turkic languages should be united into
one great ensemble extending from Central Asia to the
Mediterranean. The nationalists, without renouncing the
Muslim religion or the Ottoman tradition, wanted to create a
new Turkish identity purged of all 'universalist' or 'multinational'
aspirations.

The fourth is the Europeanising and Enlightenment identity
of the intellectual elites concentrated in the city of Istanbul.
Often the descendants of Greeks, Armenians, Jews, Iranians
or Caucasians who emigrated in the nineteenth century,
these cosmopolitan and pro-Western Turks today call for their
country to become a member of the European Union. But
this same demand is also made with a very different goal in
mind, including by people who think that Turkey's accession
to the EU would be a means by which to dismantle the power
of the military and thereby to reaffirm the country's Islamic
identity.

16. Lewis, *The Emergence of Modern Turkey*, pp. 1–17.

It is certain that there exists in the Turkey of today a 'schizophrenia', or at least a 'two-sidedness', which has caused the historian Samuel Huntington to define the country as 'Janus-faced', looking two ways.[17] The city of Istanbul, a megalopolis of some 15,000,000 inhabitants, spread across its two sides, the Asian and the European, separated by the Bosphorus, expresses this two-sidedness. The inheritor of the traditions of three empires, the Eastern Roman Empire, the Byzantine Empire and the Ottoman Empire, and then later 'Turkified' with the name of Istanbul, the city is today a forward post of Turkish pan-Islamism. Istanbul was, and not by chance, the first Turkish city which, in the middle of the 1990s, voted for an Islamist mayor, Erdogan, now the Prime Minister, a member of the radical *Refah* party which was later banned.

In reality, as Alexandre del Valle has written,

> The Turks are Turks first and foremost, the former subjects of a great Muslim empire which dominated the Mediterranean, 'humiliated' the Arabs, defeated the Persians and threatened Europe for five centuries. Members of a great Turkophone ensemble which stretches from the Balkans to China and proud of the glorious pages in the history of the Sublime Porte, they are above all Turks and proud to be so. They are nostalgic for their past Islamic-Ottoman 'greatness', memory of which is alive and well.[18]

This is the people which is insistently asking to be admitted to Europe, in order to reaffirm its strength and greatness.

... except Christian identity

The territory of Turkey coincides with the geographical area which was known as Asia Minor from the fourth century onwards. There is perhaps no other region in which the word

---

[17.] Huntington 2000, p. 139. On the many identities of Constantinople, see Mansel, 2006.
[18.] Del Valle, 2005, p. 16.

of Christ was preached as much as here. Indeed, this land – as Pope John Paul II reminded us – 'saw the first . . . was where the first shoots of the Gospel sprouted'.[19] Of the fifty places the Gospel had reached by the end of the first century, twenty-four were in what is today Turkey.

Tarsus was the birthplace of St Paul who undertook a great apostolate in Anatolia, spreading the Gospel to all peoples. In Antioch there arose a flourishing community under the guidance of St Peter who was the first bishop of the town. It was here 'that for the first time the disciples were called Christians'.[20] The Christian community of Ephesus owes its foundation to St Paul and, according to tradition, St John the Apostle governed it for many years. The same St John accompanied the Virgin Mary to Ephesus, who concluded there her earthly life in a house which is today venerated by the Muslim Turks who call it *Meryemana*, House of Mary, Mother of God. The mystery of the divine maternity of Mary was solemnly professed and proclaimed precisely in Ephesus, at the Ecumenical Council held there in 431.

The churches of Alexandria Troas, of Laodicea and of Hierapolis, where St Philip the Apostle died, are mentioned in the letters of St Paul. The churches of Smyrna, Pergamon, Sardis, Philadelphia, Thyatira, Ephesus and Laodicea, the 'seven churches of Asia', are those to whom St John was instructed to send his Book of Revelation.

The first seven Ecumenical Councils of the Church were held on the territory of today's Turkey, starting with the Council of Nicaea in 325, where the form of the Creed was formalised against the Arians. In today's Turkey the Church constituted itself and was organised around bishops like St Policarp of Smyrna and St Ignatius of Antioch; it was defended by the great Fathers of the Church from Cappadocia – Basil, Gregory of Nazianzus, Gregory of Nyssa and St John Chrysostom. Cappadocia, in the very heart of the Anatolian peninsula was, until the invasion of the Seljuk Turks,

[19.] John Paul II, 2001.
[20.] Acts, 11:26.

home to a flourishing monastic life, as testified to this day by the extraordinary complex of churches carved out of the rock.

Pope John Paul II was therefore right to call Turkey 'an authentic 'Holy Land' of the early Church, rich with a cultural tradition whose numerous traces attract the attention of the Catholic Church and of all Christians'.[21] For more than a millennium, Turkey was a Christian land. Today, however, the one identity which the Turks have struck out of their historical memory is that which refers to Christianity. Indeed it is precisely in opposition to Western Christian civilisation that the Turks have for centuries defined their strong Islamic-Ottoman identity which still characterises them to this day.

[21.] John Paul II, 1994.

Chapter Two

The European Union and Turkey

The application for EU membership

The European Union is a *sua generis* supranational institution, which was created by the Treaty of Maastricht dated 7 February 1992. Since 1 January 2007 it has been composed of twenty-seven member states. The principal organs of the EU are the European Council, the Commission, the European Court of Justice, the European Parliament, the Council of Ministers and the European Central Bank. The Treaty of Lisbon, signed on 13 December 2007, represents the EU's 'constitutional charter'.

The process of European integration has, to date, greatly weakened the sovereignty of the nation-states who belong to it without succeeding in making the EU into a major player on the international political stage. More than being a 'super-state', the EU is a hybrid organism, lacking its own political and cultural identity.[1] This weak European 'identity' has been elevated to the status of a theory by some fashionable exponents of post-modern thinking like Edgar Morin, Massimo Cacciari and Jeremy Rifkin.[2] The same 'weak' identity is supported by the majority of Europe's heads of state and government with a few rare exceptions. The decision not to insert any reference to the Christian roots of Europe in the

[1] de Mattei, 2006.
[2] Rifkin, 2004.

draft European constitution approved in 2004, or in the Lisbon treaty of 13 December 2007, is a significant expression of the loss of identity which characterises the EU.

By contrast, the Republic of Turkey has an extremely strong politico-religious identity and it has applied for EU membership not in order to renounce this identity or to dilute it but instead to impose it on the European continent.

Turkey's first step towards Europe goes back to September 1959 when the country applied for an Association Agreement with the European Economic Community. After a few years, in 1963, a treaty was signed (the Ankara Agreement) which provided for the gradual creation of a customs union with the EEC. But just as the customs union was coming into being, the military occupation of Cyprus in 1974 and the military coup of 1980 seemed destined to distance Ankara from Europe for ever.

When parliamentary rule was restored in 1987, Turkey embarked once again on her path to Europe. On 14 April 1987, the Prime Minister of the Republic of Turkey, Turgut Özal, submitted, for the first time, a formal application to join the EEC. In the meantime, the European Union was born out of the EEC. After having voted in favour of the customs union on 6 October 1999, the European Parliament voted by 259 votes for, 187 against and 84 abstentions – and thanks to support by the majority of Socialists and a minority of Christian Democrats – in favour of 'the right of Turkey to apply for EU membership'. The resolution stated that 'Ankara's accession would be an important contribution to the development of the EU, as well as to peace and security.'[3] Two months later, at the Helsinki summit on 10 December, the European Council agreed to give Turkey the status of 'a candidate country destined to join the Union on the basis of the same criteria applied to the other member states'. In December 2004 the calendar of negotiations was laid out and they are currently under way.

[3.] *Corriere della Sera*, 7 October 1999.

Respecting the 'Copenhagen criteria'

In order to join the EU, Turkey has to demonstrate that she meets the criteria laid down at the Copenhagen summit in 1993 for the accession of new member states. These principles were inserted into the Treaty Establishing the European Union by the Treaty of Amsterdam in May 1999 and they were reaffirmed in the Charter of Fundamental Rights and Freedoms approved by the European Council at Nice in December 2000.

The so-called 'Copenhagen criteria' require that candidate states have a market economy capable of competing within the European space and stable political institutions which guarantee democracy, the rule of law, human rights, freedom of religion and the respect and protection of minorities.

The European Union does not seem to be interested in the great religious and cultural questions which were put onto the world political agenda after the terrorist attacks of 11 September 2001, but only by the problem of how Turkey can meet the Copenhagen criteria. There are other problems connected with this which remain at the centre of international attention: the recognition of Cyprus, the question of the 'Armenian genocide' and the problem of the Kurdish minority.

The cost to Europe of the Turkish economy

The most attentive scholars of contemporary Turkey have noted that the current budget of the EU is not suited 'to any economic relationship beyond a simple one of free trade based on the basis of common standards of liberty and democracy'. Its economic system has all the characteristics of a backward and underdeveloped economy: low per capita GDP (€5,900 as opposed to the European average of €21,400); high foreign debt (for thirty years Turkey has been one of the four most indebted countries in the world with debt amounting to some 90% of GDP); a high tax burden (the government takes 27% of GDP in direct taxes, and if one adds the 15% budget deficit one gets to public spending of some 42% of GDP, dedicated above all to financing the army and the debt – all this without any real system of social security); permanent economic crises; inflation of 65% on average for the last thirty years; a drop in GDP of 7½% since 2001; and a total public debt of € 145 bn, equivalent to 92% of GDP, which is a level of debt perhaps bearable by developed countries but certainly not by developing ones.[4]

'Studies on poverty in 2006,' Philip Claeys and Koen Dillen point out, 'undertaken by the Turkish Institute of Statistics (Turkstat) in December 2007, have revealed that around 539,000 people died of hunger while some 13,000,000 Turks live below the poverty line. This is suprising for a country which has the largest army in NATO after that of the United States.'[5]

It is true that Romania and Bulgaria have a poverty level not far removed from that of Turkey but these are countries with much smaller populations than Turkey and who can be absorbed into the EU with far fewer difficulties.

The existence of these imbalances between the Turkish economy and the European economy has obvious consequences, as Claeys and Dillen again observe:

> In Turkey, the unemployment rate has remained between 8% and 10% but the labour market is in a much worse situation than is indicated by these figures. Turkey has an extremely low employment rate – some 44 or 45% of the population in 2006–7, compared to the European average of 64.3% in 2006. The Turkish employment rate is lower than that of any other EU state.

If Turkey joined the EU, the salaries and social advantages offered by other member states would constitute a formidable force of attraction for millions of Turkish workers who would come and settle in the West, taking advantage of the principle of the right to free movement which applies within the EU. This would cause social costs and unemployment to rise and productivity to fall, together with the quality of the

4. Del Valle, 2005, pp. 241–4.
5. Claeys and Dillen, 2008, p. 67.

labour force. The permeability of Turkey's borders would also encourage millions of immigrants from North Africa, Asia Minor, Lebanon, Iraq and the Turkophone states in Central Asia to come to Turkey and from there into the rest of the EU.

The cost of Turkish accession to the EU would be extremely high. Thanks to the poverty of its regions, Turkey would become the primary beneficiary of the European structural funds. In particular, her agriculture would get at least €65 bn from the Common Agricultural Policy.[6] A German study has estimated the total cost to be at least €10–11 bn , but this is probably an underestimate. According to the European Commission itself, in 2025 Turkey would receive between €22 and €33.5 bn in agricultural subsidies and regional funds.[7]

A 'democracy' which is not very democratic

The Republic of Turkey is officially governed under a constitution which was approved in 1982 and which has often been modified albeit in small ways, especially in 2001 and 2002. On the face of it, as Alexandre del Valle observes, Turkey appears to possess all the attributes of a democracy and, as such, to be unique in the Middle East if you exclude Israel.[8] In reality, the country has never really been governed democratically. Real power in Turkey remains in the hands of the National Security Council (*Milli Güvenlik Kurulu* or *MGK*), a sort of shadow government which is provided for in the constitution (Articles 118–120) and which is composed of the government and of the heads of the armed services (the five chiefs of the general staff).

The MGK is an executive organ with thousands of employees and which has a power of supervision and control over all ministries. On the basis of Article 118 of the constitution, the government is required to follow its advice to the letter in all matters relating to 'national security'. On paper the constitution guarantees the fundamental freedoms of citizens but

6. Verez and Chaponnière, 2005, p. 121.
7. Claeys and Dillen, 2008, p. 75.
8. Del Valle, 2005, p. 332.

Article 26 of the same constitution, which is also referred to in Article 18, provides that 'the exercise of these liberties can be subject to restrictions in order to protect national security, public order and collective security, the fundamental characteristics of the Republic, the indissoluble integrity of the state including its territory and the nation'.[9] However, the exception has become the rule, so much so that Professor Ahmet Insel has defined the regime in the 1990s in Turkey as 'a regime of national security'.[10]

The Turkish army controls universities via of the Council of Higher Education (YÖK); it controls the mass media via the High Council of Radio and Television (RTUK). It is present in nearly all sectors of economic life and it runs an enormous military-industrial complex via two institutions, the OYAK (the pension funds of the armed forces) and the TSKGV (the Foundation for the Strengthening of the Armed Forces).

From the death of Atatürk to this day, the army has used this power above all to guarantee secularism in Turkey against attempts to Islamise the country by means of the democratic vote. In spite of attempts to adapt its legislation to European standards, the Constitution of 1982 remains one of the most restrictive in terms of civil liberties. In the Republic of Turkey there is still imprisonment for political reasons, while torture and ill-treatment are also practised in prisons. These have been amply documented by Amnesty International[11] and Human Rights Watch.[12] The death penalty has been officially abolished but it was reintroduced in practice by a constitutional amendment and it can now be carried out 'in case of war, in case of the imminent danger of war or for acts of terrorism'.[13]

The new Turkish penal code (Articles 301–312) punishes even more severely than the previous one those who exercise their right to demonstrate peacefully or to express their dissent on

9.   Carducci and Bernardini d'Arnesano, 2008, p. 60.
10. Quoted in Bozarslan, 2006, p. 101.
11. Amnesty International, 2007.
12. Human Rights Watch, 2008.
13. Del Valle, 2005, pp. 97–101.

important national questions (the withdrawal of the Turkish army from Cyprus, separatism or on the recognition of the Armenian genocide). In particular, Article 301 says that 'Any person who publicly denigrates Turkishness, the Republic or the Grand National Assembly of Turkey will be punished by a prison term of between six months and three years.' In April 2008, the word 'Turkishness' in Article 301 was replaced by 'Turkish nation' and the maximum term of imprisonment was reduced from three years to two but the substance has not been changed. The 2007 report of the European Commission is extremely clear:

> The number of persons prosecuted has almost doubled in 2006 with respect to 2005 and the number of trials has risen again in 2007. More than half of these prosecutions are in respect of the Penal Code and in particular Article 301 which punishes anyone who denigrates Turkishness.[14]

The Commission's report concludes that the Turkish legal system does not guarantee freedom of expression in Turkey according to the standards of the European Union.

Turkey has been condemned numerous times by the European Court of Human Rights, the judicial authority whose seat is in Strasbourg and whose role is to ensure respect for the European Convention of Human Rights. In 2005 the Court handed down 290 rulings on Turkey in 270 of which the country was deemed to have violated the Convention.[15] This puts Turkey in first place among all the forty-five members of the Council of Europe in terms of human rights violations, even though those members include Armenia, Azerbaijan, Georgia, Moldavia and Ukraine, all countries which have all been judged to have insufficient democratic standards to qualify for EU membership. The most common judgements against Turkey concern violations of the right to a fair trial and of the right to property.

The EU demands that the military apparatus, which today guarantees the partially secular state, be dismantled if Turkey

---

[14.] European Commission, 2007.
[15.] Carducci and Bernardini d'Arnesano, 2008, p. 19.

is to be allowed to join. If this happened, the power of the military would be replaced, at least in part, by Islamic power. To an extent this has already happened. Democracy would in this case be destined to undergo a different but no less oppressive form of limitation which would affect above all freedom of religion and freedom of expression.

The Cyprus question

A serious problem which remains unresolved is that of Cyprus.

The Republic of Cyprus is a former British colony which became independent in 1960. On 1 May 2004 it joined the EU. Turkey refuses to recognise Cyprus and continues the illegitimate occupation of part of its territory, which it invaded in July–August 1974.

The origins of the conflict lie in the Treaty of Zurich and London signed by Britain, Greece and Turkey in February 1959 and by means of which Britain gave Cyprus independence but imposed on it an unworkable constitution. The Cypriot people were divided along ethnic lines into two communities: the Greek Cypriots making up about 80% of the population and the Turkish Cypriots less than 20%. The Turkish minority obtained rights which were greatly out of proportion to their real weight, including the ability to veto laws with eight Turkish Cypriot deputies which had been voted on by thirty-five Greek Cypriot deputies and seven Turkish Cypriot ones. The constitution of 1960 was based on principles of division, not ones of cooperation and unity, and the Greek Cypriots regarded it as a diktat. Archbishop Makarios (1913–1977), the first president of the Republic, tried to put the new constitution back on the table but in vain. When in July 1974 Makarios was overthrown by the Greek colonels and replaced by a puppet president, Nicos Samson, Turkey – with the tacit assent of the United States – occupied the Northern part of the country corresponding to 38% of the whole island and proclaimed an autonomous Turkish Cypriot state.[16]

16. Basri Elmas, 1998, pp. 127–42; O'Malev-Craig, 2005.

In November 1983 the Turkish Republic of Northern Cyprus was proclaimed. Only Turkey recognises this entity whose declaration of independence has been judged 'invalid from the juridical point of view' by Resolutions 541 (1983) and 550 (1984) of the United Nations Security Council. Since then the island has been divided by a wall and projects for reunification have failed, including when they have been submitted to a referendum as happened in 2004 to the initiative launched by the UN Secretary General, Kofi Annan. In the meantime, on 1 May 2004, the Republic of Cyprus was admitted to the European Union.

Today, as Alberto Rosselli observes,

> If Turkey recognised the Republic of Cyprus, it would implicitly delegitimize the government in the North. At the same time, if the EU negotiated the accession of Turkey, it would be in the embarrassing situation of supporting a state which had invaded another.[17]

The Turkish invasion left a long trail of death and destruction in its wake as well as the flight of more than 200,000 Christian Greek Cypriots to the South. The occupied territory has been subject to a strong Islamisation consisting of the destruction of everything that was Christian, as well as in a modification of the natural landscape by carving a vast crescent and star on the slopes of Mount Pentadattilos.[18]

Cyprus, the home of the oldest Christian community on European soil, has been badly wounded in its artistic, cultural and religious heritage. Byzantine and Romanesque churches, monasteries, mosaics and frescoes of inestimable value have been sacked and destroyed. Nearly all the artistic heritage of the Christian community – some 540 buildings including churches, chapels and monasteries – has been violated and disfigured.

[17.] Rosselli, 2006, pp. 84–5
[18.] Geninazzi, 2006.

A resolution of the European Parliament has given a prudent estimate of the damages:

> More than 133 buildings including churches, chapels and monasteries situated in the Northern part of Cyprus have been deconsecrated; 78 churches have been transformed into mosques; 28 are used as military stores and hospitals and 13 are used for keeping animals. Their ecclesiastical furnishings, including more than 15,000 icons, have been illegally removed and have vanished without trace.[19]

The denial of the Armenian genocide

The first genocide of modern history, after that perpetrated by the Jacobins in the Vendée in 1793,[20] is the 'Armenian genocide' (*Metz Yeghérn* or 'great evil' in Armenian).[21] The historian Yves Ternon has called it 'the prototype for the genocides of the twentieth century', the first example of the systematic destruction of a people by a state in the modern period.[22]

The Armenians are a Christian people with a rich history. They were one of the autochthonous peoples of the Ottoman Empire, together with the Greek Orthodox. Their destruction, which started in 1894–96 by Sultan Abdul Hamid II, was implemented scientifically by the Young Turks in 1915, after they had seized power in 1908–9. The presence of Armenians in Turkey, who were different from Turks in both religion and race, was considered intolerable by the new Masonic and pan-Ottoman government which wanted to create a 'Greater Turkey', purged of any trace of Christianity.

Under the pretext of their supposed 'collaboration' with Tsarist troops, the Turkish government launched a vast plan of extermination and mass deportation of the Armenian people on 24 April 1915. 'In 1915,' writes the British historian Niall

---

[19.] European Parliament, 2006.
[20.] Sécher, 1986.
[21.] On the Armenian genocide, see Impagliasso, 2000; Ternon, 2007; Dadrian, 2003; Rosselli, 2007; Flores, 2007.
[22.] Ternon, 1997, p. 167.

Ferguson, 'many places were the theatre of such ferocity that there can be no doubt about the existence of a deliberate plan for a violent "solution" to the Armenian question.'[23]

The slaughter started with the elites and the young. The men were massacred, the women were sold as slaves and shipped off into harems. Children were put into Turkish orphanages and forced to embrace Islam. Western observers like the American ambassador in Constantinople, Henry Morgenthau, wrote detailed reports about what was happening, reporting for example the declaration of the Minister of the Interior, Mehmed Talaat Pasha, saying that all Armenians had to die 'because those who are innocent today could be guilty tomorrow'.[24]

The survivors were sent by foot from Anatolia towards the deserts of Syria and Mesopotamia. In these 'marches of death' hundreds of thousands died of hunger, illness or exhaustion. Hundreds of thousands more were massacred by the Kurdish militia or by the Turkish army. Historians estimate the number of deaths at between 500,000 and 2,000,000 but the total of 1,200,000–1,300,000 is the most widely accepted figure. It is an example of 'ethnic cleansing' rarely equalled even in the barbarous twentieth century.[25]

Mustafa Kemal continued the persecution at least until 14 September 1922 when the fire and the massacre in Smyrna killed about 100,000 Greek and Armenian civilians. This was the final stage of the extermination. Alberto Rosselli writes,

Since then a veil of inexplicable silence has been cast over the first Holocaust of modern history: a massacre which with the passage of time was to be progressively forgotten about until the mid 1970s when it was finally brought back to light to be objectively examined and judged.[26]

The government of Ankara continues to deny the genocide and has threatened some countries of the European Union

[23.] Ferguson, 2008, p. 191.
[24.] Ibid., 2008, p. 190.
[25.] Lorieux, 2002, p. 71.
[26.] Rosselli, 2007, p. 69.

with 'reprisals' if they recognise it in their parliaments. Reactions in Turkey to the 'Armenian issue' are always passionate and violent and revelatory of the anti-Armenian sentiment which remains strong nearly a century after the hecatombs themselves. The Turks obstinately refuse to condemn the genocide and also persecute anyone who tries to examine objectively this tragic chapter in the history of the twentieth century.

When in February 2005, in an interview with the Swiss newspaper, *Tageszeitung*, Orhan Pamuk, who later received the Nobel prize for literature, said that in Turkey there is still silence about the massacres of the Kurdish and Armenian minorities, he was accused of 'defaming the national historical memory' and had to seek refuge in the United States.[27]

The Turkish historian, Taner Akçam, who today teaches in the United States and who is the first to have openly admitted the Armenian genocide, was arrested in 1976 and sentenced to ten years in prison for his writings; the following year he managed to flee and to seek refuge in Germany.[28]

On 19 January 2007, the Turkish-Armenian journalist Hrant Dink was murdered outside the offices of the fortnightly journal *Agos* of which he was editor. His murderers were all activists in the radical Islamic party Great Unity.[29] On 11 October 2007, Arat Dink, the son of Hrant and his successor as editor of *Agos* was given a one-year suspended prison sentence for having published in his journal an interview given by his father before his death.[30]

The request made to Turkey to recognise the Armenian genocide is not an interference in the life of this people. Germany dissociated itself from its national-socialist past and the countries of Eastern Europe who awoke from the nightmare of Communism have set up 'Museums of memory' in order not to forget their past. The German Chancellor, Angela

[27] Pamuk, 2007.
[28] Cfr. Akçam, 2006.
[29] *Le Figaro*, 21 and 31 January 2007; *Le Monde*, 23 January, 11–12 February and 3 July 2007.
[30] *Le Monde*, 13 October 2007.

Merkel, demanded in February 2009 that all Catholic bishops publicly recognise the Shoah, but no similar request has been made in the same peremptory way to the Republic of Turkey concerning the crimes of its history. Barbara Spinelli writes,

It is not acceptable that Turkey continues to honour today those who are responsible for the genocide and who defend negationist positions, when such attitudes are forbidden to the Germans. To continue to deny the genocide of the Armenians is to give Hitler a posthumous victory, since it was he who said, in August 1939, when he was warned against the invasion of Poland and the extermination of peoples, 'Who remembers today the genocide of the Armenians?'[31]

Today there are more than 6,000,000 Armenians in the world: half in the Republic of Armenia, the other half in the diaspora. However, in the eastern provinces of Turkey, which for 2,500 years were known as 'Armenia', there remains no trace of the old Christian civilisation. Caught in a vice between Azerbaijan and Turkey, and unable to count on the support of Georgia which is in conflict with Moscow, the only neighbours on whom Armenia can count are Russia and to a lesser extent Shiite Iran and Greece. Like Israel, Armenia needs the Western diaspora to survive, especially the diaspora in America and France. For the Armenians of the diaspora, as for the Jews, there exists a problem of historical identity and memory. For these people, the demand that the Turkish state recognise the genocide 'is a question of survival for their community'.[32]

The truth is that the Armenian genocide constitutes the founding act of the Turkish Republic, as indeed one of its founders, Hahil Mentese, admitted when he declared publicly, 'If we had not ethnically cleansed Anatolia of Armenian citizens who collaborated with the Russians, the creation of our Republic would have been impossible.'[33] The

[31.] Spinelli, 2004.
[32.] Ternon, 2007, p. 12
[33.] Quoted in Claeys and Dillon, 2008, p. 132.

Turkish historian Taner Akçam admits, 'The Turkish Republic was born out of the destruction of the Christian populations in Anatolia and out of the creation of a homogenous Muslim state.'[34]

The Kurdish question

There is another open wound in Turkish territory – the Kurdish question. The Kurds are an ethnic group who live in the territory known as Kurdistan which covers parts of Turkey, Syria, Iran and Iraq. It is calculated that they number 35–40,000,000 and that they are therefore one of the largest ethnic groups deprived of their national unity. Their language belongs to the Iranian stem (Indo-European family) while the majority of them are Sunni Muslims.

In 1920, the Treaty of Sèvres conceded autonomy to the Kurds but three years later the Treaty of Lausanne denied them their own state and left them under the jurisdiction of the four countries in which they lived – Turkey, Iran, Iraq and Syria. Turkey has the largest part of their territory, an area of some 230,000 square kilometres. This partition caused the birth of a nationalist movement which fought politically for the independence of the region. Atatürk and his successors saw in the Kurdish people a threat to the ethno-cultural integrity of the nation-state and tried to 'Turkify' the Kurds. The clash grew sharper in the second half of the twentieth century when the independence movement split into two wings: one national-autonomist, the other, more radical, inspired by Marxism which transformed itself in 1978 into the PKK (The Kurdish Workers' Party) of Abdullah Öçalan. The Kurds have often resorted to guerrilla warfare and terrorism while Turkey has subjected them to restrictions, often brutally. The reports of Amnesty International and of the UN have often denounced these abuses of power and the violence to which Kurdish prisoners in Turkish gaols are subject.[35]

[34.] Akçam, 2005, p. 18
[35.] Rosselli, 2006, pp. 96–100.

The problem of the Kurdish minority, like the issues of Cyprus and the Armenian genocide, are part of the 'Turkish issue' whose opening the pro-Turkish Eurocrats in Brussels repeatedly seek to delay.

Chapter Three

Christianity in Turkey: *religio depopulata*

The 'dhimmitude' of the Christians under the Ottoman Empire

Christianity, which used to flourish in the territory of Turkey, today presents the depressing aspect of a *religio depopulata*.

Before the Ottoman Empire was broken up, 30% of its subjects were Christians, nearly one in three. Today Christians represent less than 1% of the population of the Turkish Republic.[1] Responsibility for this dramatic situation goes back to the anti-Christian intolerance of Kemalist secularism and of Turkish neo-Islamism.

The Christian territories of North Africa and the Middle East were conquered by Islam from the seventh century onwards. The conquest of these territories, to which belonged three out of the four patriarchates of ancient times – Jerusalem, Antioch and Alexandria – meant that these populations were subjected to a status known as 'dhimmitude' which involved onerous juridical, religious and social limitations as well as the payment of a special poll tax, the *jizya* and a land tax, the *kharas*. They were also subject to the 'blood tax' – systematically 20% of the sons of Christians, chosen for their special beauty and strength, were forcibly converted to Islam and

---

[1] Lorieux, 2002, p. 75; Magister, 2004.

made to serve in the selected troops of janissaries. The most beautiful girls were sent to the harems.

Shariah law, a system of civil and religious law based on the Koran, was the only law recognised by the courts and the condition of dhimmitude was characterised by the denial of two essential rights: the right of self-defence and the right to testify before an Islamic court against a Muslim.[2] The *dhimmi*, i.e. those minorities subjected to this special regime, were judged according to their religious laws but these were not recognised by the Muslim courts which had primacy over *dhimmi* courts and could overturn their decisions. In daily life, Christians were subject to a subordinate code of behaviour. They were forbidden from wearing certain colours including green, the colour of Islam; they were forbidden from riding 'noble' animals like camels or horses and were allowed to ride only mules or donkeys. Bat Ye'Or reminds us that, when they were in the street, the *dhimmi* 'had to walk quickly and with a humble demeanour, they had to keep their eyes cast down and always to the left – the impure side – of Muslims, who were encouraged to push them out of the way; they had to accept insults meekly and without replying to them, and they always had to step aside for Muslims'.[3] The *dhimmi* could never exercise any authority over Muslims to whom they were always considered subject.

In countries governed by Islam, in which shariah law still constitutes the source of law – such as Egypt, Iran, Sudan, Nigeria, Pakistan and, until recently, Afghanistan – the status of Christians is inspired by the rules set down by dhimmitude, especially as with respect to laws on blasphemy, mixed marriages, apostasy, the construction or restoration of churches and religious proselytism.

[2.] Bat Ye'or, 2007, pp. 309–10.
[3.] Bat Ye'or, 2007, p. 310.

The 'Greek genocide'

In the nineteenth century, under the pressure of the European powers, the situation of the Christians in the Ottoman Empire improved and they enjoyed a certain degree of emancipation in civil, political and economic matters.[4]

In Asia Minor there were some 1,800,000 Greek Christians in about forty bishoprics and 1,700,000 Armenians in forty-six dioceses. The Catholic Church could operate with sufficient liberty thanks to the protection of the European powers, especially France. In 1912, French religious ran thirty schools in Constantinople, twenty-one in Smyrna and eighty-one in the rest of Asia Minor, with an effective influence.[5]

With the creation of Mustafa Kemal's republic, the situation worsened dramatically. A systematic programme for the elimination of Christianity was put into place.[6] The regime of so-called 'capitulations', which for centuries had governed the legal status of foreigners, and which had protected the Christians in Turkey in spite of the heavy restrictions on them, was first abrogated unilaterally in 1914 by the Young Turks and then definitely suppressed by the Treaty of Lausanne in 1923. There thus began the destruction and the deportation of religious minorities which were excluded from the new national state.

Two dramatic events, as Camille Eid reminds us, eradicated almost completely the two major Christian communities of the former Ottoman Empire: the Armenian genocide and the exchange of Greek and Turkish populations sanctioned by the Treaty of Lausanne.[7] We have already discussed the Armenian genocide but there is also a Greek or Hellenic genocide, perpetrated essentially for religious reasons.

On the eve of the First World War, the Greek Christian population of Western Anatolia and of the Pontus region

[4] Sale, 2008, p. 23.
[5] de Vries, 1944, p. 132.
[6] Lorieux, 2002, p. 61.
[7] Eid, 2006.

represented about 2,000,000 people. These were very ancient communities which had inhabited these territories for more than two thousand years, but their presence was incompatible with the ethno-religious vision of the Young Turks, which Mustafa Kemal later made his own.

The elimination of the Christians was implemented by the Turkish government even before the First World War had broken out. The historian Arnold Toynbee notes that the Turkish reprisals against the Greeks of Western Anatolia began in the spring of 1914: 'Whole Greek communities were removed from their homes by means of terrorist acts; their houses, their lands and often their possessions were confiscated and various individuals were killed in the process.'[8]

The expulsion of the Greeks from the Aegean region continued between 1916 and 1918. The Greek Christians were concentrated in groups and deported by foot towards the interior of Anatolia, using the same methods as those adopted against the Armenians. The estimates of the numbers of people who died or disappeared vary from 200,000 to 1,000,000.[9] The operation culminated, actually and symbolically, with the massacre perpetrated at the seizure of the city of Smyrna, besieged by the Turks. Mustafa Kemal's troops set light to the houses of Greeks and Armenians who tried in vain to escape towards the sea. In the port there was a score of British, American and French ships but they did nothing to receive the refugees who were slaughtered.

The metropolitan of Smyrna, Chrysostom, who was offered refuge in the French consulate, refused to save himself in order to share the fate of his own faithful. He was lynched in the public square: his eyes were put out, and his nose and ears were cut off before his throat was cut.

The massacre was witnessed, among others, by the American Consul, George Hornton, who said that the destruction of Smyrna was 'the final act in a coherent programme of exterminating Christianity within what used to be the Byzantine

[8.] Toynbee, 1970.
[9.] Akçam, 2005, p. 150.

Empire – the banishment of an ancient Christian civilisation',[10] The Christians of Pontus who survived were deported to Greece on the basis of an exchange of populations laid out by the Treaty of Lausanne. It is calculated that 1,344,000 Turkish citizens of Greek origin and Orthodox religion were forced to abandon their country to be deported to Greece, whose language they did not even speak, while 464,000 Greek Muslims were transferred to Turkey.[11] But the persecution did not stop there. In 1927 there were still 257,814 Christians in Turkey of which 178,546 lived in Constantinople, out of a total population of 13,648,270. In 1950, only 191,262 Christians remained out of a total population of about 19,000,000.[12]

In the 1930s, the process of 'Turkification' of the country undertaken by Atatürk forced the Greek Orthodox minority which had survived to emigrate. These people were part of the intellectual and economic elite of Turkey. In the 1950s the survivors were subjected to a new programme of destruction. On the night of 6–7 September 1955, the 'Turkish night', around 100,000 people armed with iron bars and divided into organised groups attacked the parts of the city inhabited by Greek Orthodox people as well as those inhabited by Jews and Armenians. The sixty-four Orthodox churches of the city, the cemeteries, schools, foundations, charitable institutions, shops and houses of Greeks were ransacked and set on fire for more than twelve hours while the police looked on. International humanitarian organisations estimated the damage at one billion lire at the time.[13] Ten years later, in 1965, some 12,000 Greek citizens living in Istanbul were expelled on the pretext that they were spies or *personae non gratae*, and their property was confiscated for the umpteenth time.

We do not have exact statistics but it is estimated that there are now about 100,000 Christians in Turkey, nearly all in the major centres of Istanbul, Smyrna (Izmir) and Mersin. A good

---

[10.] Ferguson, 2008, p. 195.
[11.] Sale, 2008, p. 25.
[12.] de Vries, 1953, col. 625.
[13.] Carducci and Bernardini d'Arnesano, 2008, p. 116.

half of them belong to the Armenian Church; there are about 25,000 Catholics with six bishops; about 10,000 Syrian Orthodox; about 5,000 Greek Orthodox; and about 3,000 Protestants of various denominations.[14]

The religious minorities in Turkey today include the monophysite Armenian Church; the Greek Orthodox Church represented by the Ecumenical Patriarch in Constantinople; the Assyrian Church of Nestorian origin; the Jacobite Syrian Orthodox Church the seat of whose patriarch is in Damascus; and the Catholic Church which has six dioceses in Turkey, three of the Roman (Latin) rite, one of Chaldean rite, one of Armenian rite and one of Byzantine rite. For these minorities the juridical basis continues to be the 1923 Treaty of Lausanne which is still applied restrictively to the Armenian Orthodox, Greek Orthodox and Jewish religions alone.

The Western rite Catholics are foreigners without the slightest juridical status or personality, as are the members of the Eastern rite churches (Assyro-Chaldean, Syriac and Maronite). Such churches do not have the right to own or manage their own educational or social institutions or even seminaries; they do not have the right to build churches. Jobs in the public sector (in the police, the army and the senior ranks of the civil service) are not open to Christians. The religious minorities are also not represented in parliament, something which prevents them from defending their collective interests and those of their members. The 2008 report on religious liberty produced by Aid to the Church in Need has documented this situation well.[15]

Turkey defines itself as a secular republic whose constitution guarantees the equality of all citizens before the law 'without distinction of opinion or religion' and which solemnly proclaims 'the freedom of worship, religion and thought'. But every day new events confirm that there is no real freedom of religion in the country. Article 24 of the constitution of 7 November 1982 affirms that 'everyone has total freedom of

[14]. Magister, 2004; Eid, 2006,
[15]. ACS, 2008, p. 511.

conscience, belief and religious conviction' but in reality full
liberty is in fact accorded only to citizens of the Muslim faith.

Anti-Christian intolerance

On 6 February 2006, Father Andrea Santoro of the Diocese of
Rome, who was involved in inter-religious dialogue, was
murdered while praying in the Church of Santa Maria in Trebi-
zond on the Black Sea, in the north of the country.[16]
According to witnesses, his murderer shot him several times in
the back while shouting 'Allah is great'.[17] In Izmir, a Slovene
Franciscan, Father Martin Kmetec, was attacked by a group
of young Muslims while inside the parish church of St Helena
on 4 February 2006. They threatened to cut his throat and
said, 'Sooner or later we will kill all of you.'[18] On 11 March 2006
a Turkish Capuchin priest received death threats.[19] On 2 July
2006, the French priest, Pierre Brunissen, was stabbed in
Samsun on the Black Sea by Muslim fundamentalists.[20]

On 18 April 2007, in the centre of Anatolia, three Evangel-
ical Christians (two Turkish converts and a German) had their
throats cut after being tortured in their place of work, the Zirve
publishing house, which defends the Bible and Christian literature. The presumed murderers, who were aged between
nineteen and twenty, belonged to a Sufi confraternity.[21]

On 16 December 2007, an Italian Capuchin, Father
Antonio Franchini, rector of the Sanctuary of the Virgin Mary
at Ephesus, was wounded by a young man with a knife as he
left the Church of St Anthony in Izmir, where he had just celebrated Mass.[22]

The Ecumenical (Greek Orthodox) patriarch Bartholomew I,
for his part, is still waiting for the Greek Orthodox seminary on

---

[16.] Cf Santoro, 2007.
[17.] *Le Figaro*, 7 February 2006.
[18.] *Zenit*, 12 February 2006.
[19.] ACS, 2008, p. 513.
[20.] *Zenit*, 2 July 2006; *Le Figaro*, 4 July 2006.
[21.] ACS, 2008, p. 513.
[22.] ACS, 2008, p. 514.

the island of Heybeliada near Istanbul to be reopened after it was closed down in 1971. Even though he has spiritual authority over millions of faithful throughout the world, for the Turkish state the Ecumenical Patriarch is only the patriarch of Fener, the name of the part of Istanbul where he has his base.

The voices of Catholics go unheeded

In Turkey, according to Father Bernardo Cervella, director of *Asianews*,

> The Christians live in a situation of dhimmitude. The problem in Turkey lies with its version of the separation of religion and the state, which is only an appearance because in fact religious liberties are denied. The state tramples on the rights of Christians while conniving with the Muslims.[23]

In an interview in *Avvenire* on 7 February 2006, the president of the Turkish Bishops' Conference, the Archbishop of Izmir, Mgr Ruggero Franceschini, said,

> In theory there is freedom of worship but in practice we face numerous limitations. We can celebrate Mass only inside churches while religious meetings in private houses are regarded with suspicion. But above all the lack of any juridical status makes it de facto impossible for the Church to own the buildings in which services are held in the same way as other kinds of property. We are not able to undertake restoration work or to build new churches. It is forbidden to open seminaries. Any religious vocations have to be pursued abroad. We cannot open schools or form youth groups because this would be seen as a form of proselytism which could endanger public order. Christians are not allowed to join the army or to have a career in public life.

The same archbishop said in 2007 that behind the acts of violence and murder perpetrated against Christians in Turkey

---

[23] *Il Foglio*, 10 February 2006.

there lay 'a culture of the exultation of the race and a false understanding of secularism'. He said,

> If they were true secularists, they should respect at school anyone of a different faith. In reality, we are faced with many years of teaching in schools which exalts Turkey, not its history or countryside but rather its military conquests. Koranic education is also obligatory in all schools, and it is very often undertaken by people who are not trained for it. Most of the teachers spend their time denying the reality of Christianity or to diminishing its value, [treating the Gospel as] an invented story.

In the same way, says the Archbishop of Izmir,

> The media in Europe are ill informed about this fundamental long-term indoctrination of hatred, of violence, of opposition which can explode at any moment, since there are no common rules – not even in civil and penal law.

In addition, the prelate says that,

> It is not in fact true that only 1% of the population of Turkey is of a different race or religion. Many people hide their religious faith and their ethnic background and accept that 'Turkish-Muslim' be written on their identity cards. Only the most courageous do not hide their identity. We can therefore say that in Turkey the percentage of those who are neither Sunni Muslims nor Turks is higher than 1%.

In Turkey it is almost impossible to obtain permission to build or restore a Christian religious building. Travelling through many cities and villages, one can see that nearly all churches have been transformed into museums, mosques, schools, libraries or barns.

The Holy See has often protested about this to the Turkish government, condemning acts of discrimination against Catholics and against other Christian minorities.

'In Turkey,' Pope John Paul II said to the new Turkish ambassador on 7 December 2001, 'Catholics are a small minority.

They are waiting for the juridical status of the Church to be recognised.'
During the visit made by the present Pope to Turkey (28 November–1 December 2006) Benedict XVI reminded the Turks about their obligations in the area of religious liberty in his speech to the diplomatic corps (28 November 2006):

> The fact that the majority of the population of this country is Muslim is a significant element in the life of society, which the State cannot fail to take into account, yet the Turkish Constitution recognizes every citizen's right to freedom of worship and freedom of conscience. The civil authorities of every democratic country are duty bound to guarantee the effective freedom of all believers and to permit them to organize freely the life of their religious communities.

The Catholic Church has asked in vain for the Turkish government to give it the right to carry out its ministry freely. Unfortunately the reforms which have been implemented, or simply announced, in the context of Turkey's accession to the European Union, have made not even the slightest hint towards the principle of religious liberty.[24]

[24.] Sale, 2008, pp. 33–5.

Chapter Four

Turkey between secularism and Islamism

The myth of 'secular Turkey'

During the fifteen years of his leadership of Turkey, Mustafa Kemal Atatürk tried to suppress the country's Ottoman identity, transforming it into a nation-state like those which came into being in the West after the French Revolution. After having abolished the Sultanate and the Caliphate, Kemal closed the Ottoman courts, Koranic schools and religious confraternities (1925); he abolished the fez for men and the veil for women (1925); he introduced a new Civil Code which was inspired almost word for word by the Swiss civil code, which abrogated the Muslim shariah (1926); he recognised civil marriage celebrated by a public official (1926); he introduced the Latin alphabet for Turkish and abolished the Arabic alphabet of the Koran (1928); he changed the weekly day of rest from Friday (the Muslim day of prayer) to Sunday (1933); he gave women the vote and made them eligible to stand as candidates in national elections (1934).

This package of reforms has been defined as a process of 'secularisation'. In reality, as the German scholar, Reinhard Schulze, has pointed out, the process was instead a profound 'Turkification' of the ancient Ottoman society.[1] Some Muslim Turks at the time understood the Kemalist reforms as a 'de-Arabisation' of Turkish Islam, a means to rediscover the true

[1] Schulze, 2004, p. 85.

'Islam of the Koran'. The reforms were said to have allowed Turkey to 'purify' the Islamic tradition from the legalist influence of the Muslim clergy, the *ulema*, who had suffocated Turkish national identity.

In fact Mustafa Kemal affirmed the primacy of the Turkish national state over the Islamic religion of the Ottoman tradition, without separating religion from politics. It should be recalled in this respect that in Islam the Christian and Western distinction does not exist between religion and politics. Consequently, as Bernard Lewis emphasises, 'The identity between religion and power is indelibly imprinted on the memory and conscience of the faithful by the sacred texts, by history and by experience.'[2]

Kemal did not want to separate religion from the state. Rather, he introduced a 'reinterpretation' of Islam in such a way as to reconcile its faith with the principles of secular nationalism which had grown up in Europe in the nineteenth and twentieth centuries. In particular, for Kemal, 'Secularisation did not mean distinguishing or separating the areas of competence of the two powers according to the European model, but instead simply eliminating religion from the political sphere and subjecting worship to the tutelage of the state.'[3]

The sentiment of belonging to Turkey was what characterised the new Turkish nation, but in order to be Turkish one first had to be Muslim. 'In other words,' observes the sociologist Hamit Bozarslan, 'secularisation became a new common denominator for the Turkish nation only as a complement to the Turkish character of Islam.'[4] The state became the holder of absolute sovereignty with a view to creating a 'national religion'.

In keeping with these principles, in 1924 Mustafa Kemal created an Office of Religious Affairs, the *Diyanet*, which reports directly to the Prime Minister and whose role is to regulate and administer all religious questions. Turkey thus

2. Lewis, 1991, pp. 279–80.
3. Mango, 2004, p. 129.
4. Bozarslan, 2006, p. 42.

became a Muslim state which subordinated religion to political power, while in the Ottoman period it was rather politics which was absorbed by religion. Like many Muslim regimes in the twentieth century, as Bozarslan observed, the Kemalist regime found in Verse IV, 59 of the Koran its favourite religious quotation: 'O, you who believe! Obey God, obey the Prophet and obey those in authority!'[5]

To this day, the Office of Religious Affairs, created to defend the secular state, exercises rigorous control over the religious life of the country. Over time, however, and above all from the 1990s onwards, the *Diyanet* has played a different role from that which it had originally. Whereas at first it depended on the government, today it has become an autonomous institution which exercises a strong influence over the politics and culture of the country. From an instrument of the 'secularisation' of Turkey, it has become the principal factor in its 're-Islamisation'.[6]

It is no coincidence that Turkey, supposedly a secular state, is today one of the countries in which the greatest number of mosques are being constructed and in which Islamic parties have the best results in elections. The re-Islamisation of Turkish society can be seen at all levels. Turkey today has 90,000 imams paid for by the state and 85,000 active mosques; one for every 350 citizens. This is the highest per capita number of mosques in the world.[7] In parallel with the reappearance of the veil in public, the muezzins' call in Arabic, which was forbidden under Mutafa Kemal, now marks the days for Turks living under the shadow of the minarets.

Muslim brothers and Sufi confraternities

In the middle of the twentieth century, Kemalism enjoyed strong influence in the Arab world. Habib Bourgiba (1903–2000) in Tunisia, Reza Khan Pahlavi (1877–1944) in Iran and Amanullah Khan (1892–1960) in Afghanistan adopted

5. Ibid., 2006, p. 43.
6. Basri Elmas, 1998, pp. 191–5.
7. Sharon and Krespin, 2009, pp. 55–6.

various reforms in their countries which were inspired by the religious-political system of Atatürk. However, these modernising and Westernising reforms provoked violent reactions in the Islamic world, above all by the movement known as the 'Muslim Brotherhood' founded by Hassan al-Banna (1906–1949) in Egypt in 1928, which campaigned for a return to the Koran or to the sunnah (the way and manners of the prophet) and to the system of shariah law derived from them.[8] While Mustafa Kemal invented the theory of 'national' Islam, reduced to the private sphere, al-Banna proclaimed that 'Islam is a complete organisation which encompasses all aspects of life ... It is faith and adoration, fatherland and nationhood, religion and state, spirituality and action, Koran and the sword.'[9]

Mustafa Kemal's reforms failed to deeply transform Turkish society. Instead, it has been progressively penetrated by Islamism. The governments which succeeded one another in the 1950s and 1960s were forced by social pressure to legitimise declared Islamist parties as political movements. The coups d'état which occurred in Turkey to restore 'Kemalism' failed to prevent the re-Islamisation of society. The military coup of 1980 was even itself a stage in this process of Islamisation, because it set down 'the Turkish-Islamic synthesis' as the new ideological basis of national unity.[10]

Throughout the 1960s, Turkey grew ever closer to the Muslim world, even through its participation in international Islamic organisations. Thus on the occasion of the World Muslim Congress which met in Mogadishu in December 1964 and January 1965, the brother states adopted a resolution in favour of the Turkish arguments about the Cyprus conflict. Ankara, for its part, regularly supported resolutions which condemned the occupation of Arab territories by Israel and associated itself with all the resolutions of the United Nations which recognised the PLO.

[8.] On the Muslim Brotherhood, see Mitchell, 1993; Pacini, 1996; Lia, 1998.
[9.] Ramadan, 2004, p. 257.
[10.] Basri Elmas, 1998, pp. 183–97.

The progressive re-Islamisation of Turkey has occurred mainly thanks to the influence of the Muslim Brotherhood and to Islamic confraternities (*tarika*), who have returned to the political stage after having been banned by Mustafa Kemal. *Naqshbandiyya* and *Sülemanciyya* are the two most influential confraternities in Turkey. Strongly opposed to Kemalism, they constitute a central element of Turkish Islam, controlling large sectors of the daily press with a total print run of 800,000 copies of which the dailies *Zeman* and *Türkye* have 300,000 each.[11]

The confraternities adhere to the initiate doctrine of Sufism, the 'mystical way' of the Islamic religion. However, like the Muslim Brotherhood, they fight for the extension of shariah law to the whole planet and for the unification of Islamic states under the authority of a restored Caliphate. 'Beyond the spiritual differences between Sufism and Sunni orthodoxy,' says Arthur du Plessis, 'one bond unites them: the conviction that the whole of humanity will eventually accept to submit itself to the shariah and that it is necessary to work ceaselessly for this goal.'[12]

The supporters of the rebirth of Islam

Three Turkish prime ministers have come from Sufi confraternity circles: Türgüt Özal, Necmettin Erbakan – the founder of the *Refah Partisi* (the Welfare Party) – and the current Prime Minister, Recep Tayyip Erdogan, who also comes from Refah and who later created the new party, *Adalet ve Kalkinma* (Justice and Development) better known as AKP.

Türgüt Özal (1927–1993) was the first promoter of the rebirth of Islam in the 1980s. He was prime minister twice between 1983 and 1989 and president of the Republic from 1989 until his death. In 1983 Özal created a large conservative party founded on the Turkish-Islamic synthesis, known as the Motherland Party (*Anavatan Partisi*), which won the first elections organised after the coup d'état of 1980. While in office, Özal,

[11.] du Plessis, 2005, pp. 51–5; Del Valle, 2004, pp. 113–18.
[12.] du Plessis, 2005, p. 98.

who was the brother of the head of the *Naqshbandiyya* confraternity and himself a member of it, abolished Article 163 of the Turkish penal code which prohibited Islamic parties and introduced a law which punishes insults against the Muslim religion. His first official visit abroad was to Mecca, in order to demonstrate the reconciliation of Turkey with Islam. It was the same Özal who made the first official application for Turkey to join the EU in 1987.

The next and more important architect of the re-Islamisation of Turkey was Necmettin Erbakan, born in 1926, the founder of various movements and parties and who was president of the Refah party from 1987. Refah was the third great pole of Islamism according to Oliver Roy in his *Genealogy of Islamism*.[13]

Because of his Islamist ideas, Erbakan spent many years in Switzerland and Germany where he joined the Muslim Brotherhood of Sa'id Ramadan (1926–1995), the son-in-law of the founder Hassan al-Banna and the father of the more famous Tariq Ramadan. Apart from a dislike of the West, Erbakan shared with the Muslim Brotherhood a sympathy for left-wing political and economic ideas which distinguishes him from Özal, a conservative supporter of the free market.

In the December 1995 election, the *Refah* (Justice) Party won a handsome victory. In June 1996, after extensive negotiations, Erdogan was asked to form the first Islamist government in Turkish history. The day after his government won its vote of confidence, 8 July 1996, the semi-official daily of *Refah*, *Milli Gazete*, announced triumphantly, 'After nearly a century in which the enemies of Islam have reigned, today begins the reign of believers.'[14]

Erbakan hoped for an 'Islamic NATO' as an alternative to the Western one, he preached the re-conquest of Jerusalem, and he claimed that Turkey had regained 'its rightful role as guide of the Muslim world'.[15] These declarations alarmed the

---

[13.] Roy, 1995, pp. 32–40.
[14.] Cit. in Basri Elmas, 1998, p. 204.
[15.] See *Corriere della Sera*, 29 June 1996.

Kemalist military which put a sudden end to his government on 28 February 1997.

Erbakan was forced to ban his own party and then to resign. At this point, within his own movement, a new current of 'young people' started to make way, led by the mayor of Istanbul, Recep Tayyip Erdogan, the third protagonist of the Islamic rebirth of Turkey.

Born in Istanbul in 1954, Erdogan made his political career in Erbakan's *Refah* Party where he was noticed for his strong Islamist positions. In 1995, just after becoming mayor of Istanbul, he compared his victory to the conquest of Constantinople in 1453. He suggested twinning Istanbul with Mecca and financing municipal voyages to Mecca and Medina in order 'to reconcile the country of Atatürk with Islam'. On 28 and 29 May 1996, while still mayor, Erdogan organised a large Islamic meeting in Istanbul whose theme was the need for Muslims to create a 'Muslim common market' and a 'Muslim United Nations' which would not be subject to the West. On 28 June 1998 he was sentenced to ten months in prison and stripped of his civil rights on the basis of Article 312 of the Turkish penal code for 'incitement to religious hatred'. This was after reciting in public, the previous December, verses from the poet Ziya Gökalp, which say, 'The minarets are our bayonets, the domes are our helmets, the mosques are our barracks and the faithful are our soldiers.'[16] Today he is the head of the Turkish government.

The AKP of Erdogan and Gül

His imprisonment and the collapse of *Refah* caused Erdogan to understand that he had to follow a different path. After an interregnum (1998–2002) in which the socialist Bülent Ecevit was in power, the Turkish Islamic movement divided into two parties in November 2002, the *Saadet Partisi* (Felicity Party) of Necmettin Erbakan and the AKP (Justice and Development Party) of Recep Tayyip Erdogan, which adopted more moderate positions. The AKP won a relative majority (34.2%) of votes and an absolute majority of parliamentary seats (363 out of 550).

Immediately after his victory, Erdogan tried to secure for himself the support of the West, sending reassuring messages to the United States and Europe and announcing that he wanted to 'accelerate Turkish candidacy for European integration'. 'We will strengthen the economic integration of Turkey with the rest of the world,' said the Prime Minister, declaring that he was 'determined to apply the economic programme together with the International Monetary Fund'.[17] In intern-al politics, Erdogan said that the AKP never had any 'religious orientation' and promised 'not to create tensions in Turkey'. He guaranteed that 'there would be no repetition of 28 February', an allusion to the coup d'état of 1997.[18]

Erdogan's strategy was clear. In order to avoid what had happened in 1997, when the army forced Erbakan to resign, it was essential now to weaken the power of the army, and only the pressure of the European Union was in a position to do this.

The objective of joining the EU presented a double advantage: the AKP could be presented as the Islamic equivalent of the 'Christian Democrat' parties and of the friends of the West, and to use the EU and its demands about 'democratic standards' as protection against the ever present threat of a new military coup.

Faced with Erdogan's reassurances, the European Commission said it was 'ready to cooperate' with the Justice and Development Party. In the West, and especially in the United States, people watched the AKP with great interest as a new experiment rooted in Sufi Islam and in part opposed to Arab Islam.[19]

[17] Agence France-Press, 4 November 2003.
[18] Agence Anatolia, 4 November 2003.
[19] Introvigne, 2006, pp. 122–5.

After the 2007 elections

Erdogan's main efforts in his first term were to accelerate Turkey's accession to the EU. These efforts culminated with the official opening of accession negotiations in December 2004.

In the elections held on 22 July 2007, the Turks confirmed the AKP in power by electing an Islamic parliament in which a two-thirds majority now governs the country as if it were a one-party state. Premier Erdogan suggested to the Members of Parliament that they elect his party comrade, Abdullah Gül, president of the Republic, who also comes from an Islamist background.

Gül's election on 28 August 2007 as the eleventh president of the Republic of Turkey signified a further collapse of one of the bastions of secular Turkey. Gül, a disciple of Erbakan, in whose government he was Deputy Prime Minister and minister of foreign affairs, is the first Islamist head of state in the eighty-four years of the history of secular Turkey.

A lucid commentator for *Il Giornale*, Marcello Foa, has explained the situation well:

> The AKP party of Prime Minister Erdogan and Gül has a double agenda. There is an openly modern economic and strategic agenda which applies rigorously the reforms proposed by the International Monetary Fund, liberalising the economy, reinforcing links with the USA and accepting the conditions laid down by Brussels to continue the accession negotiations. But there is also a second agenda which the political class and the European media refuse to see. The Turkish Islamists have changed their tactics. Until the end of the 1990s, they aimed at subverting the rigorously secular constitution created by the founder of the Republic, Kemal Atatürk, eighty years ago. But the army prevented them from doing this. They lost battle after battle. Then they understood that there exists a more effective and non-violent instrument for bringing Turkey back onto the path of the Koran – Islamisation by stealth. Rather than subverting the constitution they have started to empty it out progressively from the inside by relying on the silent transformation of social customs. This is much more effective than a

revolution. In the last five years, the number of Muslim schools in Turkey has risen, as has the number of women who wear the veil (NB This includes the wife and daughter of Gül – RdM.) Entire cities now respect Ramadan and forbid alcohol in public places, while in the civil service officials whose faith is proven are those who get promoted. Travelling in Turkey today one can see that the modern and genuinely secular areas are limited to the tourist centres on the coast and to the centres of large cities like Istanbul, Ankara and Izmir. Elsewhere the real Turkey is becoming more and more Muslim.[20]

One of the main figures of Sunni Islam, the Tunisian Islamic leader, Rashid Ghannouchi, who is also from the Muslim Brotherhood, describes the strategy of Erdogan's AKP thus:

Is it still a Muslim project? The answer is that the project consists in replacing extremist secularism with a moderate secularism in which the state remains neutral with respect to religion. It is the same project but the system is softer. It is necessary to give in on certain points from time to time without giving up what is essential ... In this country, national unity was threatened because the attempt was made to base it on nationalism imported from the West rather than on Islam. Pray to God with me that this group which has come into the very heart of our great Muslim community be given the means to realise the hopes we have placed in it.[21]

Behind Erdogan and Gül there stands the worrying figure of Fethullah Gülen, a leading Islamic thinker who left Turkey in 1998 for the United States from where he runs an international network which includes thousands of schools, universities, student residences, foundations and associations in about ninety countries.[22] Gülen is a follower of Sheikh Sa'id Kurdi (1873–1960), also known as Sa'id-i Nursi, the founder of the Islamist movement Nursi.[23] Like the leaders of the AKP,

20. Foa, 2007.
21. Ghannouchi, 2003.
22. Sharon and Krespin, 2009; Ansaldo, 2008.
23. Vahide, 2005.

Erdogan and Gül, who support him, Nursi calls for Islam to come out from the mosques and to regain its public role in society. His ambitious goal is the Islamisation of Turkey and the 'Turkification' of Islam in foreign countries.

In Turkey, Gülen's movement, which is protected by Erdogan, controls charitable organisations, estate agencies, printing presses and more than a thousand schools. The historian Michael Rubin has compared his influence in Turkey to that of Khomeini in Iran, claiming that Gülen himself could be the man who would deliver the *coup de grâce* to secularist constitutionalism.[24]

The 'party of the veil'

Bassam Tibi, a well-known Muslim scholar of German origin, has called the AKP 'the party of the veil'. The party of Erdogan and Gül, indeed, 'uses the veil as one uses a symbol. And it intends to use it towards Europe, in order to separate the system of values from the economic system . . . The European illusions about shared values are very successful in press conferences; and the fact that they are accepted by many shows the current weakness of Europe and its crises of identity'.[25]

The decision taken by the Turkish parliament on 9 February 2009 to lift the prohibition on the veil which had been in place since the time of Kemal Atatürk, and which is considered a pillar of state secularism, is for Tibi a symbol of the 'Islamisation by stealth' which threatens Turkey's entry to Europe. At the same time, the crisis unleashed in Turkey on 14 March 2008 by the chief prosecutor of Ankara who denounced the AKP and seventy-one of its leaders for their 'anti-secular' activities, eventually came to nothing when the case was quashed. On 5 June the Constitutional Court restored the prohibition of the veil in universities but it refused to ban the AKP, limiting itself to cutting public finances.

[24.] Rubin, 2008.
[25.] Tibi, 2008, p. 95.

Recep Tayyip Erdogan and Abdullah Gül insist they are not Islamists and that they support both Kemalism and the European Union, but it is worrying that they also demand that their wives and sisters wear the veil. This is the reason why in June 2004 both men did not bring their respective wives to the official reception on the occasion of the NATO summit even though they had been invited by the president, Ahmet Sezer.[26] In reality the veil, which is prescribed by shariah, has become not only a flag of identity for the AKP but also the political symbol of radical Muslims in Europe. The great relevance of the phenomenon lies in the fact that it has gone beyond the confines of Turkey and even of the Muslim world.

Tibi points out that in the large urban centres of Turkey you do not see as many veiled women as you do in Germany or in other European countries.[27] In the societies of south-east Asia, for example, where Islam is the largest religion, if a woman wears the veil she is immediately labelled as an Islamist.[28]

In Europe, the veil is an ideological barrier which proclaims the existence of an inviolable screen of separation between Islamic society and Western society, a symbol of struggle brandished in the name of the refusal to integrate. The argument over the veil which has been going on in Turkey since the 1980s therefore has implications which extend far beyond a simple discussion about clothing. These implications do not concern the Muslim world alone, because through Turkish immigration and the eventual accession of Turkey to the EU, this conflict could spread like wildfire on the European continent.

[26.] Ibid., p. 42.
[27.] Ibid., p. 163.
[28.] Ibid., p. 197.

Chapter Five

Islam and Europe

The 'Islamic club' – the Organisation of the Islamic Conference

It would be short-sighted and simplistic to discuss the problem of Turkey's accession to the EU without putting it in the historical context of the relationship between Europe and Islam. For Turkey, even after the fall of the Ottoman Empire, has never renounced its Islamic identity. On the contrary, this identity has become ever stronger since Erdogan and Gül came to power.

To raise the question of Turkey's Islamic identity is not an attempt to widen the question of its EU accession inappropriately from politics to religion. On the contrary, the fact cannot be ignored that in addition to the history of Turkey, the country today is more religiously homogeneous than any European country. This is because the number of Christians living in Turkey is smaller than the number of Muslims living in any French *département* or in any European region.[1]

Before they applied to join the EU, the Turkish Islamists were strong opponents of it. They called the EU 'a club of Christians which wants to dictate Turkey's politics to her'.[2] Today, this phrase, originally coined by Islamist anti-Europeans, has been appropriated by pro-Turkish pro-Europeans who say that

[1] Besançon, 2003.
[2] Basri Elmas, 1998, p. 209.

Europe should open herself to Turkey and thereby cease to be 'a Christian club'.[3]

In reality, twenty-seven European states belong to a 'club' which has deliberately removed all reference to Christianity from its founding charter. Neither in the original proposal for a European constitution, drawn up by the European Convention in 2003, nor in the modified version of it known as the Treaty of Lisbon of 2007, does there exist any reference to the Christian identity of Europe. This removal of the historical memory of Europe has a symbolic importance, as has been noted, which is far greater than would have been the case if there had been some reference to Christianity in the constitutional text.[4] In spite of the repeated calls of Popes John Paul II and Benedict XVI, by also of many intellectuals – including Christians and those without faith[5] – the European Union chose to define itself as a explicitly 'secular' club if not 'secularist'.

There is, however, a rigorously 'Muslim club' of which Turkey is a member; the Organisation of the Islamic Conference (OIC), the largest inter-governmental organisation after the United Nations.

The OIC is an international organisation founded on 25 September 1969 at Rabat in Morocco to which fifty-seven countries from the Middle East, Africa, Central Asia and the Indian subcontinent belong. Since 2004, its General Secretary has been a Turk, Ekmeleddin Ihsanoglu, a historian of Islamic science who is one of the 138 signatories of the open letter 'A Common Word Between Us and You', dated 13 October 2007, which was written in response to the speech given by Pope Benedict XVI at Regensburg on 12 September 2006.

The name 'conference', and the variety of the Islamic states who belong to the OIC, suggest the idea of a plurality of positions and currents. However, one cannot apply to the OIC the criteria which apply to international organisations of

---

[3.] See for example The Daily Telegraph, 12 July 1999.
[4.] Weiler, 2003; de Mattei, 2006.
[5.] See for example, Weiler, 2003; Pera and Ratzinger, 2004.

Western origin like the UN or even the EU. The common element between the member states of the OIC is the Muslim religion. What unites them is the sense that they belong to a single community, the *Umma*, which includes not only Muslims who live in Islamic countries but also those who live in any other part of the world, including Europe.

The purpose of the OIC is to preserve and defend Islamic identity against the Western word, which is considered to be 'the house of the infidels'. The OIC does not recognise the Universal Declaration of Human Rights but instead the Cairo Declaration on Human Rights in Islam, approved at Cairo on 5 August 1990 on the occasion of the nineteenth Islamic conference of Foreign Ministers. Article 24 of this Charter says, 'All the rights and freedoms stipulated in this Declaration are subject to the Islamic shariah.'

In December 2005, the OIC met in Mecca and gave itself a series of objectives including the Palestinian question; the need to build the unity and solidarity of the *Umma* by spreading the Koran and the *Sunna*; the fight against Israel; support for Muslim minorities in Europe; the fight against Islamophobia at the international level by means of education and communication. Anti-Zionism, anti-Americanism and anti-Christianism are the three pillars of this political vision. This explains why the world conference of the UN 'against racism, xenophobia and slavery' which was held in Durban in the summer of 2001 was transformed under pressure from the OIC into a veritable anti-Western *J'accuse* which passed over the real forms of slavery and intolerance which are widespread above all in Muslim countries. The Western branch of the OIC is the international organisation 'Alliance of Civilisations' created in September 2004 by the Turkish Prime Minister Erdogan and his Spanish colleague, José Luis Zapatero. The report prepared by the High Level Group of the Alliance of Civilisations on 13 November 2006 promotes the OIC's policy in relation to Israel and Europe according to the same basic themes.

The first idea of creating the Alliance of Civilisations goes back to when the then president of the Islamic Republic of

Iran, Mohammed Khatami, convinced the member states of the OIC, at its meeting in Tehran in 1999, to adopt a project of 'dialogue between civilisations' in response to the 'clash of civilisations' about which Samuel Huntington had written.[6]

Khatami's project, put forward by the OIC and then picked up by the 'Alliance of Civilisations', is based on one guiding principle: that the principle of multiculturalism and of cultural relativism, a principle which is rejected in Islamic countries, should be adopted by the post-Christian West in order to allow Muslim minorities there to extend the Islamic shariah in a peaceful and progressive way by means of the weapon of 'dialogue'.

From the principle of multiculturalism flows the promotion and the defence of Islam in the West, and the denunciation of all forms of discrimination towards Muslims as well as of all attempts to integrate their identity in the West. In February 2008, Prime Minister Erdogan, on a visit to Germany, and speaking in the stadium at Cologne to more than 20,000 Turks, called their assimilation in Europe 'a crime against humanity'.[7]

The first disadvantage of multiculturalism, observes Marcello Pera, is that it has caused 'a guilt syndrome' to be born and to develop among Europeans.[8] Faced with the demands of minorities of all types – ethnic, religious and cultural – the culture of the host society withdraws and loses its own identity. Furthermore, multiculturalism creates a strong nexus between ethnic identity and cultural identity and leads to the creation of a multitude of ghettos which an 'enlightened' Muslim like Bassam Tibi calls 'parallel societies'.[9] The creation of these parallel and conflictual societies is encouraged by the fact that in Islam identity is not personal, as in European culture, but instead collective. The call of the Umma, the Islamic religious community, retains all its influence over the fragile psychology of people who have

6. Bensimon, 2008; Bat Ye'or, 2008; Markovich, 2008.
7. FAZ.net (Frankfurt), 10 February 2008.
8. Pera, 2008, p. 118.
9. Tibi, 2003, pp. 158–85.

been uprooted.[10] These people often live in urban areas which have been transformed into 'free zones' not subject to state control. These zones end up enjoying a sort of extra-territorial status, becoming zones of lawlessness in which state laws are replaced by the ethno-religious juridical codes of the community.[11]

The ethnicisation of Islam, which is caused by multicultural-ism, produces an explosive mix in the hands of deracinated people of the second and third generation, and opens up the perspective of a series of civil wars in Europe.

The multiculturalism of the 'Alliance of Civilisations' in reality risks leading to a clash of civilisations within Europe itself.

'Jihad' and 'Egira' as strategies of conquest

At the centre of Islamic civilisation from its very origins lies the concept of *jihad* or 'holy war', the juridical-theological doctrine which obliges every Muslim to fight to defend and spread Islam all over the world.[12] This doctrine distinguishes *dār-al-Islam*, the 'territory of Islam', in which the Muslim reli-gion reigns, from *dār-al-harb*, the territory populated by infidels, against which war is obligatory for as long as they refuse to recognise the sovereignty of Islam, which in its orig-inal sense means 'submission'. This war does not need to be declared because there is no other relationship possible between two opposed worlds. Whoever opposes the spread of Islamic law (the shariah) is considered as 'an enemy'. But those who accept the Muslim conquest are recognised as *dhimmi* or *zimmi*, infidels 'protected' by the *dhimma*, a treaty of surrender which subordinates protection to the choice of submission to Islamic domination.[13] In Islamic countries, Bernard Lewis points out,

---

[10.] Ibid., pp. 107–8.
[11.] Vignelli, 2002, pp. 103–4; Pera, 2008, pp. 114–20.
[12.] On *Jihad* see de Mattei, 2001; Charnay, 2003; Bostom, 2005; Sookhdeo, 2007; Cook, 2007.
[13.] Bat Ye'or, 2007, pp. 29–30.

The fundamental political, social and even economic classification has been Muslim, Zimmi, Harbi. This three-way division between believers, unbelievers who have been subjugated and enemy unbelievers has been far more important than the subdivision between Turks, Persians and Arabs in Asia.[14]

Europe, inhabited by 'infidels', is 'the House of War' *par excellence*. Every European is considered *harbi*, an enemy of Islam, if he has not converted to Islam or accepted the condition of *dhimmi*. The category of 'Islamophobia' includes the *harbi*, that is all those who reject the alternative between conversion to Islam and dhimmitude. In Europe, the territories which were occupied for a while by Muslims are considered the property of Islam in perpetuity. Spain, for example, which was conquered for several centuries by Islam, is considered to be an Islamic territory called Al-Andalus which Muslims have the duty to re-conquer. The same can be said of the city of Jerusalem. Muslims do not accept that a territory in which the Jews were *dhimmi* like the Christians today can have dominion over the Muslims.

The conquest or re-conquest of European territories also occurs by means of immigration. *Egira* or migration, which takes its name from the first 'migration' of Mohammed from Mecca to Medina, is indeed in Islam a form of *jihad*, the name of the 'force' used to implant universal Islam.

In Islamic doctrine, as Bassam Tibi reminds us, *jihad* and *egira* are two complementary concepts. In Arabic, migration is translated as *egira,* a term which does not indicate only geographical or physical moving but which also has a religious connotation. The calendar of *egira* starts with Mohammed 'migration' from Mecca to Medina in the year 622: this is the Year 1 in Islamic chronology. From this, the term *egira* is linked to that indicating the expansion of Islam in the world.

Egira is therefore not only the movement of an individual or a group of individuals from one place to another, but the

14. Lewis, *The Emergence of Modern Turkey*, p. 329.

missionary duty to spread Islam which can be done within a non-Muslim nation either by means of violence or peacefully, like propaganda (da'wah).[15] The Koran, in Sura 8:72, recalls 'those who believe and who migrated and fought for Islam with their goods and their souls for the cause of Allah'.

The doctrine of egira is equivalent to an expansion in Europe of the dar al-Islam and it coincides with what Bat Ye'Or calls 'soft jihad', a cultural war different from 'hard jihad', Islamic military war.[16] One can also make the distinction between a 'Gramscian' Islamism and a 'Leninist' Islam. Leninist Islam is that of those Muslims who want to conquer Europe using the instruments of war and terrorism. Gramscian Islamism is that of 'moderate' Muslims who want to achieve the same goals by means of demographic growth, the Islamisation of public life and the introduction of Islamic law into Western institutions. It is also expressed by means of intimidation and threats within Islamic communities towards those who criticise even a few aspects of Islam. Between these two currents, 'moderate' and 'radical', there are in fact no differences over goals but only over the strategy by which to achieve them.[17]

Islamo-Gramscianism or 'soft-jihad' was theorised from 1974 onwards at the Second Islamic Conference in Lahore, when the then Secretary General of the Islamic Conference, Muhammad Hasan al-Tuhami, proposed creating cultural centres and universities all over the world to spread Islam by means of debates, meetings, conferences and publications.[18] This developed under the aegis of the Muslim Brotherhood which created cultural centres and Islamic banks all over Europe to finance the activities of da'wah. Whereas Islamic Leninism is that of Osama Bin Laden and the 'jihadists', Islamo-Gramscianism is well represented by the activities of the Muslim Brotherhood and of personalities such as Tariq Ramadan, the grandson of the founder of the Muslim

[15.] Tibi, 2003, p. 160.
[16.] Corrispondenza Romana, 22 March 2008.
[17.] de Mattei, 2001, pp. 69–70.
[18.] Bat Ye'or, 2007, pp. 72–4.

Brotherhood Hassan al-Banna.[19] Reconstituting his grand-
father's thought, Tariq Ramadan reminds us that he has no
doubt that Islam, sooner or later, will be reborn and that its
civilisation will provide the world with the solutions which today
it cannot find . . . The promise of the Koran, the reawakening
of Islamic peoples, the decline of the West, the law of time –
all this leads to the same conclusion: the future belongs to
Islam'.[20]
Mosques play a central role in the Muslim Brotherhood's
system of conquest. According to Magdi Allam, the Muslim
Brotherhood 'promotes the Islamisation of society from the
bottom up, via control of mosques, of Islamic cultural
centres, or Koranic schools, of charitable foundations and of
financial institutions. The strategy pursued is that of gradually
bringing an Islamic state into being within the democratic
state'.[21] In Islam, which has no specifically priestly function
and therefore no true divine worship, the mosque plays the
role of community assembly, for Koranic teaching and for
political and cultural propaganda. It is the centre for spreading shariah, the Islamic law. Sheikh Yusuf al Qaradawi, in a
fatwa on 29 October 2001,[22] stated that 'The mosque has
always played a role in jihad in the name of Allah, to fight the
invaders, the enemies of this religion.'

Turkish immigration into Europe and 'the people of the mosques'

The movement which has put down the deepest roots
among Turkish immigrants in Europe is l'*Avrupa Milli Görüs
Teskilatari* (AMGT), an organisation whose name in Turkish can
be translated as 'the national point of view'. It was founded in
1970 by Necmettin Erbakan, after his Islamist party was
forbidden by the Constitutional Court of Turkey and he sought

[19] See also Besson, 2005; Landau, 2005; Vidino, 2006; Murawiec, 2008, pp. 32–7.
[20] Ramadan, 2004, p. 357.
[21] Allam, 2005, p. 22.
[22] Quoted in Solomon and Alamaqdisi, 2007, pp. 39–40.

asylum in Germany and then Switzerland. Erbakan gave the organisation two goals: the re-Islamisation of Turkish immigrants who were in contact with 'impious' Western societies, and the consolidation abroad of the base of the Islamic movement in Turkey, which was subject to repression by the authorities in Ankara.[23]

Although created by Erbakan and then headed by his nephew, Mehmet Sabri Erbakan, the European *Milli Görus* supported Erdogan's AKP when it split off from Erbakan's *Refah* party at the beginning of its ascent to power. At various elections, the European *Milli Görus*, especially the German branch, gave financial support to Erbakan's movement.

Milli Görus is present above all in Germany but also in France, the Netherlands, Austria and other European countries. It has about 300,000 sympathisers who attend the Koranic schools it controls. The association's logo shows Europe depicted in green, the colour of Islam, and framed by the Islamic crescent from Portugal to the Urals. Its principal press organ, *Milli Gazete*, defends the propaganda of Turkey and the setting up of shariah law.

The second most influential Turkish Islamic organisation within the diaspora is the Sufi confraternity, *Suleymanci*, which operates through its Union of Islamic Cultural Centres (*Verband der Islamischen Kulturzentren* in German).

Faithful to a theocratic vision of Islam, the *suleymani* oppose the 'secular' states of the West but they prefer to live under the 'infidel' laws of European states like France and Germany than under those of countries which have not yet been completely Islamicised, like Turkey, where they run the risk of being subject to restrictions.

In Germany, an ultra radical group which split off from *Milli Görus* came to light in February 2002 as it prepared suicide attacks aimed at destroying Atatürk's mausoleum in Ankara. This organisation, founded by Cemaleddin Kaplan (1926–1995) was banned by the German authorities in 1997. Today its leader is Metin Kaplan, 'the caliph of Cologne' who

---

[23.] Del Valle, 2004, p. 259.

was convicted of murdering his rival for the 'caliphate'.[24]
Unlike *Milli Görus*, which is very close to Sunni Islam and
linked to the Muslim Brotherhood, Kaplan supports the
Islamic revolution of Ayatollah Khomeini in Iran as the best
means by which to re-Islamise the Turkish and European
Muslims.

A caliphate for Europe?

The abolition by Mustafa Kemal of the Ottoman Caliphate in
1924 inflicted a deep wound, including in Turkey, which has
not yet healed. Muslim groups of all tendencies eagerly
discuss the issue of the Caliphate as the supreme authority of
Islam.[25] It is with this goal is mind that the proposal should be
understood to create a 'European imam' and a new 'social
contract' for the Muslims in Europe, a proposal which was
launched in 2007 by the international journal *European
View*.[26]

The author of the article is Mustafa Ceric who, in addition to
being the Grand Mufti of Bosnia-Herzegovina (a title which in
Sunni Islam applies to the person who has the authority to
interpret Islamic law) is also, like the Secretary General of the
OIC, Ekmeleddin Ihsanoglu, one of the 138 signatories of the
letter to Pope Benedict XVI, 'A Common Word'. The Muslim
Association of Britain awarded two prestigious prizes, the Life-
time Achievement and the Building Bridges prizes, to Ceric
and Ihsanoglu respectively, both considered 'moderate'
Muslims who support dialogue and who promote the peaceful coexistence of the Muslim population in Europe.

The question of the 'imamate' as supreme Islamic leadership, has become, according to the Bosnian Grand Mufti, the
central question for the Muslim world today, from the centre
to the periphery and including Europe. His proposal to create
'a European imam' is based on three traditional pivots of
Islamism: the concept of *aqidaha*, of *shariah* and of

[24.] Introvigne, 2006, p. 106.
[25.] Ramadan, 2004, p. 340.
[26.] Ceric, 2007, pp. 41–8.

imamah. The first term refers to the Islamic doctrine expressed by these words: 'I believe that there is no other God than Allah and that Mohammed is his prophet.' The second theological pivot is shariah, the Islamic law, which summarises the pact of Muslims with God, rather like the covenant of Moses and Jesus for Judaism and Christianity. The third concept, the *imam*, a term which is often interchangeable with the term 'caliph' (*khalifa*) is more immanent than transcendent because it refers to a human authority which acts on the basis of divine faith, representing the community gathered together in the mosque.

Ceric is one of the authors who in addition to the *dar al-Islam* (the house of Islam) and the *dar al-harb* (the house of war) admits a third category, *dar-al-sulh* (the house of the truce) which would include territories which are tributaries of Islam and which have signed with it a 'pact' or social contract.[27] For the Grand Mufti, Europe is not *dar-al-Islam*, the house of Islam, and it is not *dar-al-harb* either, the house of war. Europe is *dar-al-sulh*, the house of the social contract. But the Islamic social contract coincides with shariah, the pact with Allah, which is 'non-negotiable' because it derives from an infinite God and is not terminable. The idea of an Islamic 'social contract' is accompanied by the proposal to create an imam who would represent all the Muslims of Europe and who would be able to negotiate the contract with European political authorities.

In Europe, according to Ceric, there are some 30,000,000 Muslims who are divided into three large groups: indigenous, immigrants and natives. The indigenous are those Muslims who have historic roots in Europe like those of Bosnia, Albania, Kosovo, Macedonia, Bulgaria and so on. The immigrants are those who after having emigrated as students or workers have settled in the states of the EU. Finally the natives are the children of Muslim émigrés but also those Europeans who have recently converted to Islam. All these groups have in common the law of the Koran, even if they differ from each

27. Gardet, 1981, pp. 26–7.

other in their experiences and in their expectations.

According to Ceric, the indigenous Muslims defend their religious and cultural continuity; the émigrés want to overcome their status as foreigners; the natives and the converts to Islam want to preserve their identity. In all cases they identify with Islam. The Grand Mufti has not restricted himself to asking that these people have the same rights as Europeans; he is calling for the application of Islamic law itself. He writes, 'It is now time that we seriously consider a way to institutionalise the presence both of Islam as a universal religion and also of Muslims as global citizens.' The imam should represent the voice of Muslims in their dual role as believers in Islam and citizens of Europe. The creation of an 'imamate' understood as both a political and religious authority, which would represent the whole of the Muslim community, is considered by Ceric to be an opportunity not to be lost in order to legalise shariah in Europe, and to overcome the current divisions within Islam, above all between Sunni and Shia Muslims.

In the last two centuries, Europe has undergone a process of secularisation which has deprived the Catholic Church and the other churches of all direct relationship to political power. But while Europe has cut all forms of institutional links between Church and State, the Grand Mufti of Bosnia wants to make the Continent religious again in the name of a tradition and a culture which are in fact opposed to that of the West. The final words of his article sound indirectly threatening: 'As for European society, it is also still too immature to comprehend the significance of a single Muslim authority for the sake of overall European peace and security.'

It should be recalled that the imam or caliph is not only a religious authority but also a political one, because Islam absorbs politics within religion. The imam, indeed, does not restrict himself to being the voice of a religious faith, because that would presuppose accepting the Western distinction between Church and State. He is also the political representative of the community which lives according to the Islamic law. But is this law compatible with democracy? Is Islamic family law, for instance, compatible with European family law? It is not clear why Muslims, as citizens, should be represented by an imam and not by the democratic institutions of the states in which they live, which are organised around rules and procedures shared by all states in the EU. European Islam would have a representation which is politically and culturally different from the democratic standards currently in force, if not even opposed to them. What support would Turkey give to these proposals once it had become a member of the European Union?

Chapter Six

The geopolitical scenarios: the 'zone of tempests'

The two directions in which Islam expanded

Islam developed in a region of Central Arabia, the Hedjaz.[1] From there, it spread rapidly throughout Mesopotamia, Syria, Egypt and Iran. The centre of the Muslim world is still in isthmus regions, between the Persian Gulf, the Red Sea, the Mediterranean, the Black Sea and the Caspian Sea. From this region, throughout the course of history, Islam has projected itself towards the West in order to subjugate it to the law of the Koran. The expansion of Islam to Europe took place along two main axes and it was conducted by two different peoples, the Arabs from the south-west and the Turks from the south-east.

Having conquered North Africa, the Arabs invaded Spain and crossed the Pyrenees before being stopped by Charles Martel in 732. From then on they withdrew progressively before being finally expelled from the Iberian peninsula in 1492. The Turks, having conquered the Byzantine Empire and parts of the Habsburg Empire, were stopped at Vienna in 1683. In this case, too, the military defeat of Islam was a turning-point which caused it to lose territories progressively in Central Europe.

Today, the Muslim offensive on Europe's borders is taking place in the same two directions. In the south-west, by means

[1] Cfr. de Planhol, 1968.

of the creation of 'Eurabia':[2] an area of socio-economic osmosis and of cultural intermixing which is supposed to unite North Africa (the Maghreb and the Mashrek) with Southern Europe. The cultural, religious and educational action promoted by the European institutions is a central element in this Euro-Arab synergy. The pretext of 'Islamophobia' is used to isolate any form of resistance to the Islamisation of the European continent.

In the south-east, the line of attack is the entry of Turkey into the European Union, a political movement which, in addition to opening the door to an unstoppable Muslim migration to Europe, would also overturn the balance of power within the EU institutions. In both case, the geopolitical consequences would be explosive.

A geopolitical revolution

Geopolitics is the science which studies the balance of power between states and regions. In the fullest sense of the term, it needs to take ethnicity, language and culture into account and to consider the deep relationships which exist between peoples and civilisations. Turkey, from the geopolitical point of view, constitutes a junction between three geo-cultural regions in the world – Europe, the Middle East and Central Asia. In these regions its interests contrast with those of Russia and with the ancient Christian civilisations of the Caucasus, who are also turned towards Europe.

If one was to lay down an order of priority among the various interlocutors of the West in this region of the world, then one would put Georgia and Armenia in first place, linking them to other countries which are Christian and European like Ukraine and the Baltic states; in second place one should take post-Soviet Russia into consideration, for this country is also Christian but of a more Asiatic than European tradition. Turkey ought to come last since she is extraneous to Europe by her religious history and by her political geography. The

---

[2.] Bat Ye'or, 2007.

choice of the United States and the European Union seems unfortunately to be the opposite of what it should be, and the Christian countries of the Black Sea are therefore often sacrificed to Turkish and Russian interests in the region.

Many people are convinced that Turkish accession to the EU would allow the West to control the oil and gas resources of the Caspian Sea and Central Asia, as well as the waters of the Gulf and the Near East. In particular, successive American governments have been in favour of Turkish accession to the EU because they think of it as an important strategic pawn on the 'great chessboard' of the Middle East.[3]

After the end of the Second World War, Turkey joined NATO (in 1952) and provided a large contingent of soldiers. As Samuel Huntington observes,

> Turkey became the recipient of billions of dollars of Western economic and security assistance; its military forces were trained and equipped by the West and integrated into the NATO command structure; it hosted American military bases. Turkey came to be viewed by the West as its eastern bulwark of containment, preventing the expansion of the Soviet Union toward the Mediterranean, the Middle East and the Persian Gulf.[4]

Huntington also reminds us that the accession of Turkey to the West was a product of the Cold War. The end of this period, according to the American political scientist, removed the principal justification for this, weakened this link and brought about a need for it to be redefined.[5] Turkey's readiness to collaborate with the West in confronting Islamic terrorism has certainly been shown to be far weaker than that which it displayed when opposing the Soviet threat.

The collapse of the USSR has indeed caused a genuine geopolitical revolution, in which Turkey has assumed a new role. The 'pan-Turkic' ideology, which had been shelved by

---

3. Brzezinski, 1998.
4. Huntington, 1997, p. 144.
5. Ibid., p. 145

Mustafa Kemal, has now returned to the political scene, where it operates side by side with neo-Islamism, with the support of some American analysts who have encouraged Ankara to play the role of a dike in the region against Islamic 'fundamentalism', in order to protect the well-being of the West, by means of oil and gas networks.[6]

On 18 November 1999, in Istanbul, with the support of President Clinton, an agreement was signed between Turkey, Georgia and Azerbaijan for the construction of an oil pipeline from Baku to Ceyhan, which was intended to become the principal outlet for oil from the Caspian Sea. The intention of the Americans was to isolate Iran, a country which, like Turkey, had been considered a faithful ally of Washington until the sudden arrival to power of Khomeini. But, as the political scientist Srdja Trifkovic observes,

> What will happen if history repeats itself, if Ankara goes the way of Tehran, cutting off American's access to the oil-rich Caspian region and bringing into its orbit America's new clients in Sarajevo, Tirana and Pristina? Is it possible, or likely, or even imminent? Can the U. S. afford to be caught by surprise yet again? What can it do to prepare for such eventuality? (...) The same dynamics that have swept it away in Tehran may apply in Ankara. The parallel with Iran is alarming.[7]

The pan-Turkic Utopia

It should not be forgotten that alongside the religious role of Islam there is the geopolitical role of pan-Turkism. If we look at the countries which have been dominated by the Turks from the sixteenth century to our own day, we see an immense empire which embraces large parts of Asia, all of the North African coast and the Middle East, and which extends to the very borders of Italy and Austria.[8] The spreading of Turkic languages is a testimony to the expansion of this empire –

6. Vielmini, 1999.
7. Trifkovic, 2002, pp. 239–41.
8. Pitcher, 1972, Map V.

some thirty linguistic systems in a territorial continuum which extends from the Balkans to Central Asia.[9]

It was on the basis of this ethno-linguistic reality that the pan-Turkic ideology was born in the nineteenth and twentieth centuries. Its origins lie in the studies of Armin Vambery (1832–1913), a Hungarian-Jewish linguist, who put forward the theory that the Turkish and Hungarian languages share a common origin. From these theories emerged Turanism, an ideological current which proposed the reunification of all the 'Turanic' peoples (Finno-Ugric, Turkic and Mongol). Pan-Turkism, of which Turanism was the political version, was advanced above all by the 'Young Turks' movement.

A call for the unification of Turkish-speaking peoples as the precondition for their cultural *risorgimento* was also made in the late nineteenth and early twentieth centuries by the Crimean Tartar scholar, Ismail Bey Gaspirali (Gasprinski) (1844–1914) who in 1907 founded the Union of Muslims. Its goal was to unite all the people of Islamic faith within the Russian empire.

The father of Turkish nationalism, Ziya Gökalp (c.1875–1924), was also inspired by these ideas. He called for the right to extend the 'political borders' of the Turkish fatherland to wherever its 'languages and cultures' extend.[10] He called for the restoration of the lost empire in Europe and the Balkans between 'all those who share the same race and religion as the Turks'.[11] 'The nation of the enemy' he proclaimed, 'will be destroyed, Turkey will be great and will become Turan.'[12] (Tur is the legendary ancestor of the Turks who fought against the ancestor of the Arians). Turan was also an imaginary place, the ideal fatherland, 'the sum of all nations in which Turks live and in which Turkish is spoken'.[13]

The pan-Turkists dreamed of creating an Altaic-Turkish

9. Banfi and Grandi, 2004, pp. 68–74.
10. Quoted in Akçam, 2005, p. 73.
11. Ibid., p. 143.
12. Ibid., pp. 143–4.
13. Ibid., p. 143.

empire from the Mediterranean to China, and of which Ankara would be the centre. Mustafa Kemal opposed such foolish ambitions but pan-Turkism was re-born after the Second World War and especially in the 1980s when it converged with neo-Ottoman Islamism.[14] Out of this meeting between political Islamism and pan-Turkism emerged the 'Islamic-Turkish synthesis', which both the national-conservative right and the Islamists made their own. It is important to recall, however, that the Ottoman Empire never extended into Central Asia to the East of the Caspian Sea, and that the supporters of pan-Turkism therefore rely on ethno-religious considerations rather than on religious ones, unlike the neo-Islamists and the neo-Ottomans.

Formed at the beginning of the twentieth century, as the Ottoman Empire was collapsing, pan-Turkism found in Ismail Enver Pasha (1881–1922) one of its greatest exponents. He was a protagonist of the Young Turks Revolution and an architect of the Armenian genocide. When in 1996 Enver's body was discovered in what is today Tadjikistan – he died during a conflict with the Red Army – the Prime Minister, Necmettin Erbakan, was there to welcome the triumphant return of his remains to Turkey and elevated him to the rank of national hero. Today the pan-Turkic ideology is professed not only by extremist groups like the 'Grey Wolves' – to which Mehmet Ali Agca belonged, the man who tried to Kill Pope John Paul II – but also by a large part of the Turkish political class.

It was from the 1990s onwards that the Turks started to suggest to their '200 million co-nationals' in the Turkophone states of the East the idea of setting up 'a community of states from the Adriatic to the Great Wall of China', according to the expression used by the Prime Minister, Turgut Özal,[15] who loved to speak of a 'Turkish world' and of the coming of a 'Turkish century'.

The five new states which have come into existence following the dissolution of the Soviet Union – Azerbaijan,

14. Del Valle, 2004, pp. 223–4.
15. Zürcher, 2007, p. 397.

Turkmenistan, Uzbekistan, Kazakhstan and Kyrgyzstan – form the nucleus of this Turkophone community. From the beginning of the 1990s, and under Özal's presidency, Turkey tried to fill the void created in these states by Moscow's withdrawal, intervening in the economy, religion and culture and using instruments like radio, television and satellites.

After they gained their independence these counries underwent a massive process of re-Islamisation by means of the construction of mosques and support given for the maintenance of imams. The *Diyanet* (the state office for religious affairs) is the official body in charge of this proselytism and it has an office in every Turkish embassy. Alongside it there operates a myriad of Islamic foundations and confraternities.[16] Among the most active is *Fethullah Gülen*, the promoter of innumerable cultural institutes in which 'Turkish Islam' is taught; this runs in parallel to the Shiite Islam promoted by Iran and the Wahhabism promoted by Saudi Arabia.

The 'Turkish-Islamic synthesis' is a formula in which two identities converge: a religious identity, which draws on the Ottoman tradition, and a political identity which draws on the 'secular' nationalism of Mustafa Kemal. The 'neo-Turkists' believe that Islam, the Turkish national religion, is indispensible for cementing Turkish identity, while the neo-Ottomans see in Turkism the possibility of reinforcing the Islamic tradition by 'de-Arabising' it.

Expansion in Bosnia and the Balkans

Islamism and pan-Turkism have a strong appeal for populations in Asia but also for those in Europe who lived in the Turkish-Ottoman sphere of influence, especially in the former Yugoslavia and Albania. These areas are inhabited by a mosaic of peoples making up nearly 20,000,000 Muslims of which many are Turkophone.

For Ankara, the wars in the former Yugoslavia in the years

16. Pérouse, 1999, pp. 125–6.

1992–95 created favourable conditions for Islamo-Turkish expansion in the Balkans. Like much of this region, Bosnia was part of the Ottoman Empire until 1908. However, before the Balkan wars, according to Bassam Tibi, Bosnian Islam was a possible model for Euro-Islam, or rather for a form of non-'fundamentalist' Islam which would be compatible with Western systems. After the conflict, because of the influence exercised by Turkish and Iranian Islamists and by the so-called 'Arab Afghans' of Al Qaida, European Islam started to be abandoned and Bosnia started its slide into fundamentalism.[17]

When Yugoslavia still existed, the Bosniaks were Muslims who belonged to a specific religious community which was however made into a secular community enjoying its own political identity. The Balkan wars caused many Bosnian Muslims to think of themselves as part of the *Umma* and to proclaim their adherence to shariah law. According to Tibi, this was a Bosnian variant of the same Islam which is dominant in Turkey following the AKP's ascent to power, and which is incompatible with 'Euro-Islam' or the separation between religion and politics.[18]

Turkish influence and the progressive Islamisation of society progressed under the nationalist regime of Alija Izetbegovic (1925–2003), the president of Bosnia-Herzegovina from 1990 to 1996. This process included: the partial re-introduction of shariah law in courts of law; the Islamisation of the army and the police (90%); military cooperation with Ankara; the reappearance of the veil; the exaltation of Ottoman Turkish civilisation in school books; attacks against mixed marriages; a 'Muslim preference' for recruitment and promotion; the introduction of Arab and Turkish words into the new Bosniak language (the publication of a dictionary of 20,000 Turkish expressions); courses in Arabic and the Koran in schools; streets re-named with Turkish names; the destruction of hundreds of Orthodox and Catholic churches, and the

[17.] Tibi, 2008, pp. 197–214.
[18.] Tibi, 2008, p. 207.

expulsion of thousands of Croats and Serbs from Bosnia.[19]

In the Balkans, it has been obvious how far Turkey has been able to play on the pro-Turkish feelings of those European peoples who converted to Islam under the Ottoman Empire, and to make use of this for the purpose of its geopolitical deployment in south-east Europe. Within the geopolitical context of the geopolitical recomposition of the Balkans and of the diplomatic return of Turkey, the aim of the Bosnian and Albanian-speaking nationalist movements is to reconstruct a sort of Islamic confederation under an informal Turkish protectorate. Alexandre del Valle describes this in the following way:

> This pan-Islamist and neo-Ottoman project is called 'the green diagonal' or 'the green ridge' – the Greeks and the Slavs also call it 'the Turkish corridor'. It is indeed a Muslim geopolitical continuum which starts in Turkish Eastern Thrace and ends in the Bihac pocket, passing through Greek Western Thrace, Bulgaria and Macedonia, where there are large Turkified Muslim communities, and of course Kosovo and Bosnia, two links in the chain which have already been 'liberated'. In the medium term, the reconstruction of a 'neo-Ottoman' Islamic confederation could become a reality. The territortial continuity of the Slavo-Albanian 'green diagonal' with irredentist Turkey implies joining a part of Bulgaria – which has a large Muslim minority (12%), very closely linked to its Macedonian neighbours – to the Albanian parts of Macedonia, the Sandjak and Bosnia, and through to Albania itself, via the enclave of Gorazde and Kosovo. There thus remain hardly a hundred kilometres to re-conquer in order to obtain this geographical continuity, and to unite the Muslims of the former Yugoslavia and Bulgaria to their brothers in Turkey. An indication of things to come lies in the construction of mosques along the Serbo-Bulgarian border. This region has been abandoned by the Serbs – and the Pomak Muslims of Rodope expect to populate it soon.[20]

[19.] Del Valle, 2004, p. 226.
[20.] Del Valle, 2004, pp. 226–33.

Turkey, crossroads of criminality and drug trafficking

The abolition of border controls between the member states of the European Union and Turkey, from which hundreds of thousands of illegal immigrants come from Asia, Africa and the Muslim world, is destined to provide a major impulse for illegal immigration but also for all sorts of trafficking, from arms to drugs.

During the Balkan wars, Turkey became a transit zone for the shipment of arms from Shiite Iran to Bosnia. Alongside the Arab or Afghan volunteers who fought in Bosnia, a considerable number of Turks came to help the Bosniaks fight the Serbs.

Turkey is one of the three routes used by European Al Qaida volunteers – the first is across Syria, the second via Turkey and Kurdistan, the third is towards Southern Iraq from Kuwait and Saudi Arabia.

Turkey is also a crossroads for drug trafficking into the European market. In April 2006, the Turkish drug baron, Abdullah Baybasin, who is responsible for 90% of the heroine which enters Great Britain, was sentenced to twenty-two years in prison in London.[21] His brother, Huseyn Baybasin, whom *The Observer* called 'the Pablo Escobar of heroine trafficking' in Europe,[22] and who is serving a twenty-year prison sentence in Holland, controls from behind bars a true empire which, in addition to a series of criminal activities in England, extends into Germany, Holland, Spain and Italy.[23]

When he was arrested by the Dutch police in 2001 and charged with a series of crimes, Baybasin denied all those relating to drug trafficking saying that he was working for the Turkish government. 'I think of myself as a civil servant, a diplomat, a policeman,' he told the daily newspaper *Volkskrant*, admitting that he had become the head of the largest drugs cartel in the world only thanks to 'the full support of Turkish politicians, police officials and the Turkish secret services, the MIT'.[24]

[21.] Summer, 2006; Tendler, 2006.
[22.] *The Observer*, 17 November 2002.
[23.] *Corrispondenza Romana*, 24 June 2005.
[24.] *The Observer*, 17 November 2002.

The 'zone of tempests'

In reality, by admitting Turkey, the European Union would be importing all of this Asian country's most thorny geopolitical problems. 'All the dangers of the new world disorder are there, within a single country, Turkey ... The security of this country is a 360° nightmare,' Thomas Friedman wrote in the *International Herald Tribune* on 18 May 1995. 'Integrated into Europe, Turkey would drag Europe into its pan-Turkic policy which consists in grouping the Turkophone populations of the Caucasus around Turkey.'[25] Turkey's geopolitical sphere of influence, which extends from Bosnia to China and includes the Balkans, the Caucasus, Kurdistan, Afghanistan, Tajikistan and Chinese Turkistan, is often called 'the zone of tempests' by geopoliticians.[26] In addition, Turkey borders Iran to the east and Syria and Iraq to the south, three countries which are centres for anti-Western terrorism and Islamism, and who are home to, or who finance, organisations like Al Qaida or Hezbollah.

As Bassam Tibi points out,

> If Turkey joined the EU, with its links to the Balkans, Central Asia and the Middle East, the EU would find that it bordered regions in the world in which Islamic jihadism is growing strongly. The danger would increase that this enemy would infiltrate the EU's own territory.[27]

In other words, the 'tempests' would rage in Europe too.

[25.] du Plessis, 2005, p. 11.
[26.] Del Valle, 2005, p. 234.
[27.] Tibi, 2008, p. 214.

Chapter Seven

Benefit or catastrophe? Some conclusions

Turkey often presents her application to join the EU in an imperative manner, as if it were her given right. Erdogan has said that Turkey's accession to Europe should not been seen only in an economic light but as 'a meeting of civilisations'. 'If the EU is not a Christian club, if it is not a mere economic entity but an ensemble of political values, then Turkey should belong to it.'[1]

Faced with such an explicit request, it is often said that a negative response would cause feelings of 'rage' or 'frustration' to grow in Turkey. Further, it is added, Turkey has belonged to NATO since 1952, it was one of the first countries to join the Council of Europe and it applied to join the EU long before other member states, while some countries like Russia, even though they are closer to Europe, have never applied to join. The first reason for granting this request is said to be the very fact that it has been made.

Such a proposition discredits those who make it. It overlooks the reasons why Turkey has applied to join, and the consequences for the EU of agreeing to it. These reasons and these consequences have been the subject of this study and now is the time to summarise them.

The treaty of Lisbon, like the Treaty of Maastricht, reserves EU accession to European states. Turkey is not a European state, neither by its history nor by its geography. Its ethnic and

---

[1] Erdogan, 2004.

linguistic roots are Asian and its culture and religion are extraneous to the European tradition.

For many centuries, Europe was for Turkey a 'land of conquest'. For a while, this was a military conquest; today it is a peaceful conquest by means of penetration into the fragile and permeable institutions of the European Union.

The conquering drive towards the West is not a phenomenon of the twentieth or the twenty-first centuries but a constant in Turkish expansionism throughout the course of history.[2] Bassam Tibi defines the contemporary migration of Islam towards Europe as a third wave, after the conquest of Spain (the first wave) and the advance of the Ottoman Empire (the second wave).[3]

In the seventeenth century, the drive towards Europe by Turkic peoples was stopped by the Christian armies. But the spirit of revenge continues to find a home in Islamic nationalism. In the twentieth century of Atatürk, a nationalist poet predicted that 'one day Europe will bow before Turkey for ever'.[4]

Vural Öger, a German Member of the European Parliament who is of Turkish origin, declared during a lunch held before the European elections in 2004, 'What Suleiman started with the siege of Vienna in 1683, we will bring to fruition with our inhabitants, with the power of our men and women.'[5] He predicted that in 2100 there would be more than 35,000,000 Turks in Germany.

Thus would the aspirations be fulfilled of the spiritual father of Erdogan and Gül, Neçmettin Erbakan, who once said to a German journalist,

> You think that we Muslim Turks come here just for work and to pick up the crumbs of your money. No, we come to take control of your country and to put down roots and thus to construct what we consider appropriate, and we intend to do all this with your consent and according to your laws.[6]

2. Kinross, 2001, pp. 15–17.
3. Tibi, 2003, p. 173.
4. Quoted in Ricci, 2008, p. 9.
5. Quoted in Claeys and Dillen, 2008, p. 77.
6. Quoted in Solomon and Alamaqdisi, 2007, p. 56

The unresolved contradiction between Kemalism and Islamism

Turkey today is no longer the Turkey of Mustafa Kemal Atatürk. Nor is it that of the military officers who between the 1950s and the 1990s tried to preserve the 'Westernisation' of the country. Indeed, responsibility for the fact that Islamists have been able to win power so easily in a republic which claims to be secular lies also with the army who, on the occasion of the military coup in 1980 gave Islam an official role in public life by adopting the ideology of the 'Turkish-Islamic synthesis'.[7]

The 'secular' and pro-Western face of Kemalist Turkey no longer corresponds to daily reality in the country: from the 1990s onwards, Islamism has entered the Turkish political scene and the heads of the state and government today, Abdullah Gül and Recep Tayyip Erdogan, are two disciples of Neçmettin Erbakan, the architect of a movement of re-Islamisation which extends beyond the borders of Turkey to the whole of the Turkish emigration in the West.

The 'post-Kemalist' Turkey of today is governed by the Islamists of the Justice and Development Party (AKP). Admission to the European home is a means by which Turkey can regain its geopolitical role in those parts of the world which used to be part of the Ottoman Empire or Turkish-speaking, and above all by which it can use the juridico-political umbrella of Brussels to neutralise the hostility of the Kemalists and of the Turkish military.

The contradiction between a Kemalist identity and a Muslim one has not been resolved.[8] The European Union requires that Turkey comply with the 'Copenhagen criteria' and with Western 'democratic standards' as a condition for its accession. But the reason why Turkey today is not a fully Islamic country is precisely the authoritarianism of the army which guarantees the secular nature of the country's institutions.

The supporters of Turkey's admission to the EU claim that Turkey would be the natural ally of the West against Islamism.

7. Basri Elmas, 1998, p. 172.
8. Cf. Van Aalderen, 2008, pp. 105–13.

But inasmuch as Turkey democratises, it is destined to de-Westernise in order to embrace Islam completely. The *Refah* Party's victory in 1995 was hailed in the West as 'a perfect expression of the democratic maturity of Turkey', but in fact Europe later greeted the 'secularist' coup d'état of 1997 with a sigh of relief.[9]

The European Union would have as one of its member states a completely Islamic country, precisely thanks to its own democratic rules which in Turkey would rapidly bring fundamentalism to power. Turkey would represent an Islamic enclave in Europe, not through its immigrant minorities as is already happening today, but instead as a fully-fledged country with the same rights as the other member states of the EU.

Turkey's request to join the EU should not necessarily be interpreted as a change in its history or as a choice for the 'Europeanisation' of its customs and institutions. Erdogan's AKP does not propose to 'Europeanise' Turkey but to de-Westernise and 'Turkify' Europe.[10] There are plenty of indications that this is the case. In 1994, the Kemalist elite, which wanted to make Turkey into a 'Western' country within the Muslim world, was in favour of an agreement on military coopera-tion with Israel. In 2009, by contrast, Prime Minister Erdogan publicly quarrelled with the Israeli president Shimon Peres during a televised debate at the World Economic Forum in Davos. On his return to Turkey he was hailed as 'the new Saladin' and as the symbol of Muslim pride by a crowd waving Turkish and Palestinian flags.[11]

The demographic time bomb

The new European constitutional treaty gives EU member states a political weight proportional to their demographic weight. The population of Turkey in 2006 was 72,000,000.

9. Basri Elmas, 1998, p. 172.
10. Tibi, 2009; Id., 2006.
11. *Il Giornale*, 31 January 2009.

Although Turkey has experienced a slight inflexion in its demography, the birth rate is still 2.8 children per woman as against a European average of 1.7. According to the projections of the National Institute of Statistics, published in *Turkish Daily News*,[12] there will be 90,000,000 Turks in 2023, the centenary of the foundation of the Republic, compared to 85,000,000 Germans in Germany.

The political consequences of this demographic strength are easy to predict. As far as the EU Council of Ministers is concerned, the Treaty provides for a system of vote by 'double majority'. This means that in order to take a decision 55% of the member states (currently fifteen out of twenty-seven) must be in favour of it, representing 65% of the population of the EU. With more than 15% of the population of the EU on its own, Turkey would become a crucial factor in all decisions.

The European Parliament will have 750 members shared between states in proportion to their demographic weight, up to a maximum of ninety-six MEPs per state. The Turkish Republic would be, with Germany, the only country to have this maximum number of MEPs provided for by the Treaty of Lisbon. In order to make room for these new MEPs, the numbers of MEPs from other countries, especially the United Kingdom, France and Italy, would inevitably have to be reduced.[13]

The presence of Turkey would radically change the balance of power within the EU. With nearly 90,000,000 inhabitants, Turkey would be the most populous state in the EU with the largest number of MEPs. This would mean, as the then president of the European Convention, Valéry Giscard d'Estaing, declared in 2002, 'the end of the European Union'.[14]

On paper Turkey is a secular state. But 98% of the population is Muslim, 68% Sunni and 30% Shiite. Nor should it be forgotten that Turkey has a diaspora of more than 4,000,000

[12.] *Turkish Daily News*, 3 January 2003.
[13.] Giscard d'Estaing, 2004.
[14.] Ibid., 2002.

citizens in the EU, all of whom are Muslims. It is easy to imagine the creation of an Islamic trans-national political party which could become the largest European party and which could aim to lead the Old Continent. With or without Erdogan, post-Kemalist Turkey would assert itself as the leading country in the Islamic world within the EU, where it would be a major player.

Turkey could elect or determine the election of the president of the European Council or of the European Parliament. European politics would be subordinated to the political and religious interests of Turkish politics. It is important furthermore to consider the Turkophone inhabitants of the regions which border Turkey. Thanks to the double-nationality which Turkey gives them, these people would be able to move freely in Europe, with the same rights as European citizens. Out of a population of 470,000,000 non-Turkish Europeans in 2024, the EU with twenty-eight member states would include between 150 and 200,000,000 Turkophones, in other words one European in four would be Muslim. Turkey would co-opt Europe into her pan-Turkic policy, pushing its centre of gravity towards the Caucasus and Central Asia.

Samuel Huntington reminds us that, among Muslim countries, Turkey is the only one which can boast profound historical links with the Muslims of the Balkans, the Middle East, North Africa and Central Asia. Thanks to these links, it would be able to call itself the leader of Islam if it abandoned secularism. He writes, 'Turkey has the history, the population, middle level of economic development, national coherence, military tradition and competence to be the core state of Islam.'[15]

Europe could thereby become part of a greater Maghreb, as Bernard Lewis predicted in an interview with *Die Welt* on 28 July 2004,[16] or of that greater pan-Turkic Turkestan to which all Turkish Islamists have aspired.[17] The Islamist ideologues and the Turkish geopoliticians openly express their hope of

[15.] Huntington, 1997, p. 178.
[16.] Lewis, 2004.
[17.] Tibi, 2008.

conquering European public life, entering the EU, relying on the fact that by means of double nationality the 90,000,000 Turks of tomorrow could double in number.

The preservation of the identity of Muslim minorities in the West would be accompanied by dissolution of the identity of the West, reduced to an area of religious and cultural 'conquest'. Among Muslim immigrants (Turks, people from the Maghreb, Southern Asians) there exists the conviction that they form one *Umma* and that they should include Europe in the *dar-al-Islam*, the home of Islam. Europe and the West would thereby become 'lands of testimony' or zone of prose-lytism, an area for the expansion of Islam. It is illusory to imagine that one can neutralise this danger with 'inter-religious dialogue' with Islam, something about which Pope Benedict XVI has shown his misgivings in a letter to Marcello Pera.[18] The warning given at the Synod of Bishops in 1999 by Mgr Giuseppe Germano Bernardini OFM,Cap., Archbishop of Izmir, should not be forgotten. Mgr Bernardini told how during a meeting on Muslim-Christian dialogue, an authoritative Muslim personality turned to the Christian participants and said, calmly and with certainty, 'Thanks to your democratic laws we will invade you; thanks to our religious laws we will dominate you.'[19]

Rome, the 'Red Apple'

The two major mosques in Germany, in Pforzheim and Bremen, are named after Mohammed II, the Sultan who conquered Constantinople in 1453. The ultimate goal of the Turkish conquests, according to an ancient tradition, is called 'the Red Apple' (*Kizil-Elma*). This is the name used to denote the golden globe supported by the statue of the Emperor Constantine in Constantinople. After the conquest of the Byzantine capital in 1453, Rome became the 'Red Apple', the ultimate objective of the Ottomans and the symbol of the

18. Pera, 2008, pp. 10–11.
19. Nitoglia, 2002, p. 122.

triumph of Islam over Christianity.[20] This demand has not weakened over time. The construction in 1995 of a large mosque in Rome, the capital of Christianity, is of enormous symbolic importance.

President Nasser revealed to Cardinal Silvio Oddi that Rome was a fundamental goal for the Arab conquest.[21] Cardinal Oddi explained,

> The conquest of the Christian West, as the Egyptian president Nasser told me, is indeed one of the primary objectives of the Islamic world which now extends its influence from Asia to Africa and which is penetrating massively even into the European continent by means of the recent phenomenon of immigration. The construction of a mosque in Rome is part of this project of Islamising our society.[22]

Sheikh Yusuf al-Qaradawi, the spiritual guide of the Muslim Brotherhood, and whose ideas, broadcast in the media and on the internet, influence large parts of contemporary Islam, recalled on 2 December 2002 that when the prophet Mohammed was asked which city would be conquered first, Rome or Constantinople, he replied, 'The city of Hirquid (Constantinople) will be conquered first.' Qaradawi adds,

> The city of Hirquid was conquered in 1453 by the young Ottoman emperor of 23 years of age, Mohammed bin Murad, known to history as Mohammed the Conqueror. The other city, Rome, remains and we believe and hope [that she too will be conquered]. This means that Islam will return to Rome conquering and victorious after having been expelled twice, once from the South, from Andalusia, and a second time from the East when it knocked several times at the gates of Athens.[23]

[20.] Mango, 2004, p. 233.
[21.] *Corrispondenza Romana*, 10 June 1993.
[22.] Oddi, 1993.
[23.] Karsh, 2007, pp. 237–8.

The same Al-Qaradawi, in a fatwa promulgated on 27 February 2005 declared,

> Notwithstanding the pessimism among Muslims, at the end Islam will govern and will be the head of the whole world. One of the signs of the victory will be that Rome will be conquered, Europe will be occupied, the Christians will be defeated and the Muslims will grow in number and become a force which will control the whole of the European continent.[24]

It is not surprising that during a visit to the Dutch city of Arnhem in 1989 Neçmettin Erbakan declared openly, 'The Europeans are sick. Let us give them medicine. All of Europe will become Muslim. We will conquer Rome.'[25]

A choice of civilisations

Examining the problem of Turkey's accession to the EU, the historian Massimo de Leonardis puts the crucial question very clearly:

> The fundamental question is this: is it worth introducing into the EU a large state which certainly does not share the same historical heritage, culture or religion, in other words the civilisation of the Europeans, and whose accession would certainly force us to renounce further what remains of our Christian inheritance, all in the hope – which remains to be tested – that this will reinforce our resistance to the Islamic danger? Do we really believe that the indubitable problems which would be caused internally by Turkey's accession could be compensated by the advantages of the relationship with Islam, or that the further loss of Christian identity would reinforce Europe in that 'clash of civilisations' which, whether we like it or not, is currently taking place? To use categories used in the past with respect to socialism and communism[26], will Turkey be a barrier against Islamic fundamentalism or instead a bridgehead for Islam? The Roman Empire, the Medieval *Respublica Cristiana*,

---

[24.] Quoted in Solomon and Alamaqdisi, 2007, p. 56.
[25.] Quoted in Claeys and Dillen, 2008, p. 102.
[26.] Corrêa de Oliveira, 1982.

the Habsburg Empire, if you like the United States with its melting pot, can easily integrate different ethnic groups and cultures. But how can the European Union do it if it is deprived of its own Christian roots?[27]

To such a question we reply with the same clarity. The European Union is not in a position to integrate a nation which is as foreign to our political, cultural and religious traditions as Turkey is. Among the many identities which characterise the history of Turkey, the only one which has been completely eliminated is precisely its Christian identity – the only thing which could constitute a true cultural bridge between Europe and the West.

We do not want to deny Turkey the chance of becoming a privileged interlocutor for Europe and a geopolitical partner. But we do deny that the accession of Turkey to the European Union can represent a benefit for Europe. We believe, on the contrary, that the inclusion of 90,000,000 Turks in the political and social structures of Europe would constitute an irredeemable catastrophe for our continent.

We should add, however, that the final responsibility for this catastrophe would not lie with Turkey, which is coherently seeking and defending its own identity, but with Europe, which had abdicated its role and denied its own roots. Pope Benedict XVI has often spoken of the 'dictatorship of relativism' which is threatening a West which used to be Christian.[28] It is precisely this cultural and moral relativism which today wants to force us to accept the accession of Turkey to the EU, censuring all opposing voices in the name of 'political correctness'. It is surprising in this regard how the Turkish case is never discussed in debates in national parliaments or in the European parliament. On such an important subject which will affect the future of all of us, there should be a popular referendum, whether at the European level or in the individual nations, to find out what European citizens really think about Turkish accession. But public opinion is systematically

27. de Leonardis, 2006.
28. de Mattei, 2007.

excluded from this kind of debate, precisely because its voice would be critical towards the political class which determines the fate of Western peoples.

The words of Cardinal Josef Ratzinger on Turkey's accession to the EU

Before he became Pontiff, Pope Benedict XVI expressed his opposition to the accession of Turkey to the EU on two occasions: in an interview with *Le Figaro Magazine* on 13 August 2004, and in a speech on 18 September of the same year to the diocese of Velletri of which he was the titular. In both cases he did not express the opinion of the Holy See but his personal view.

Cardinal Ratzinger told Sophie de Ravinel:

> Europe is a cultural, not a geographical continent. It is its culture which gives it a common identity. The roots which have formed and allowed the formation of this continent are those of Christianity ... In this sense, Turkey has always represented throughout history another continent, in permanent contrast to Europe. There were the wars against the Byzantine Empire, the fall of Constantinople, the Balkan wars and the threat against Vienna and Austria. So this is what I think: it would be a mistake to treat the two continents as if they were the same. It would mean a loss of richness, the disappearance of culture in favour of benefits in the economic field. Turkey, which considers itself a secular state but based on Islam, could try to give birth to a cultural ensemble with some Arab neighbouring states, and thereby become the protagonist of a culture which would possess its own identity but which would also be in communion with the great humanist values which we must all recognise. This idea is compatible with forms of association and close, friendly collaboration with Europe, which would permit a common force to arise which would counter all forms of fundamentalism.

In his later speech to Velletri, Cardinal Ratzinger said,

> Historically and culturally, Turkey has little in common with
> Europe. It would therefore be a great mistake to include it in
> the European Union. It would be better if Turkey served as a
> bridge between Europe and the Arab world or if it formed its
> own cultural ensemble together with it. Europe is not a
> geographical concept but instead a cultural one, which was
> formed as the result of a historical development which
> included conflict but which was based on Christian faith. It is a
> fact that the Ottoman Empire was always opposed to Europe.
> Even if Kemal Atatürk built a secular Turkey in the 1920s, the
> country remains the nucleus of the former Ottoman Empire, it
> has an Islamic basis and therefore it is very different from
> Europe. Even if Europe is also a collection of secular states,
> nonetheless it has a Christian basis, however much this is unjus-
> tifiably denied today. So the entry of Turkey into the EU would
> be anti-historical.[29]

We do not believe that the judgement of Benedict XVI
today is different from that of Cardinal Ratzinger. When he
visited Turkey in 2006, the Pontiff avoided touching on this
delicate subject.[30] However the public opinion of the whole
world, and not just Catholics, regards Rome as the seat of the
supreme moral authority of humanity. Clarificatory words by
the Catholic Church should not be regarded as an interference in politics but on the contrary as a judgement on
political events expressed from the point of view of elevated
observation: that which judges history in the light of Truth, and
which takes to heart not contingent interests but instead the
perennial interests of nations and peoples.

Moved by this love for the Truth, we have written these
pages and offer them to European public opinion, entrusting
them to Her who in the dark days of humanity has always
hastened to the aid of the Christian people and who for this
reason is still venerated with the title of *Auxilium Christianorum*
– Our Lady, Help of Christians.

[29.] Ansa, 20 September 2004.
[30.] Bendict XVI, 2006.

Bibliography

ACS = Aiuto alla Chiesa che Soffre, *Libertà religiosa nel mondo. Rapporto 2008*, Città Nuova, Rome, 2008.

Ahmad, Feroz, *Turkey. The Quest for Identity*, Oneworld, Oxford, 2005 (2003).

Akçam, Taner, *Nazionalismo turco e genocidio armeno. Dall'Impero romano alla repubblica*, Guerini e Associati, Milan, 2005.

al-Quaradawi, Yusuf, *Priorities of the Islamic Movement the Coming Phase*, Awakening Publications, Swansea (UK), 2000.

Allam, Magdi, *Bin Laden in Italia. Viaggio nell'Islam radicale*, Mondadori, Milan, 2002.

——, *Kamikaze made in Europe. Riuscirà l'Occidente a sconfiggere i terroristi islamici?*, Mondadori, Milan, 2005.

Amar, Jacques, 'L'alliance des civilisations: une guerre contre soi', *Controverses*, n. 9 (November 2008), pp. 87–94.

Amnesty International, *Amnesty International Report 2007 Turkey*, www.amnesty.org

Anciaux, Robert (ed.), *La République laïque turque trois quarts de siècle après sa fondation par Atatürk*, Complexe, Brussels, 2003.

Ansaldo, Marco, 'Che fare? La Turchia in Europa ci conviene?' *Limes*, n. 5 (2002), pp. 117–20.

——, 'Fethullah Gülen primo nel mondo', *La Repubblica*, 24 June 2008.

Banfi, Emanuele & Grandi, Nicola, *Lingue d'Europa. Elementi di storia e di topologia linguistica*, Carocci, Rome, 2004.

Basri, Elmas Hasan, *Turquie-Europe. Una relation ambiguë*, Syllepress, Paris, 1998.

Bat Ye'or, *Les Chrétientés d'Orient entre Jihad et dhimmitude*, preface by Jaques Ellul, Jean-Cyrille Godefroy, Paris, 2007 (1991).

——, *Eurabia*, (Italian translation) Lindau, Turin, 2007.

——, 'Multiculturalisme et alliance des Civilisations', *Controverses*, n. 9 (November, 2008), pp. 60–86.

Benedetto XVI, *Servitori della pace: viaggio apostolico in Turchia* (28 November–1 December 2009), Libreria editrice vaticana, Vatican City, 2006.

Bensimon, Jean-Pierre, 'L'Occident et la politique d'alliance des civilisations', *Controverses*, n. 9 (November, 2008), pp. 41–59.

Besançon, Alain, 'La Turquie n'est pas Europe', *Commentaire*, n. 101 (spring 2003), pp. 177–9.

Besson, Sylvain, *La Conquête de l'Occident. Le project secret des islamistes*, Editions du Seuil, Paris, 2005.

Biagini, Antonello, *Storia della Turchia contemporanea*, Bompiani, Milan, 2002.

Bombaci, Alessio and Shaw, Stanford J., *L'Impero Ottomano*, Utet, Turin, 1981.

Bostom, Andrew (ed.), *The Legacy of Jihad*, Preface by 'Ibn Warrāk, Prometheus Books, New York, 2005.

Bourlard, Johan, *Le Jihâd. Les textes fondateurs de l'Islam face à la modernité*, Preface by Marie-Thérèse Urvoy, Editions de Paris, Paris, 2008.

Bozarslan, Hamit, *La questione kurde*, Presse des Sciences Politiques, Paris, 1997.

——, *La Turchia contemporanea*, Il Mulino, Bologna, 2006.

Bozdémir, Michel, *Turquie: entre Islam et Europe*, Ellipses, Paris, 2007.

Brandolino, Erica, 'La Corte europea dei diritti dell'uomo e l'annosa questione del velo islamico', *Diritto Pubblico Comparato ed europeo*, I (2006), pp. 97–114.

Brzezinski, Zbigniew, *La grande scacchiera*, ('The Grand

Chessboard'), Italian translation, Longanesi, Milan, 1998.

Cacciari, Massimo, *Geo-fisiologia dell'Europa*, Adelphi, Milan, 1994.

Calchi Novati, Giampaolo and Di Casola, Maria Antonia (eds), *L'Europa e i ruoli della Turchia*, Giuffré, Milan, 2001.

Caligiuri, Mario, *Prove tecniche di democrazia. Il progetto educativo di Dewey in Turchia*, Rubbettino, Soveria Mannelli, 2007.

Cantoni, Giovanni, *Aspetti in ombra della legge sociale dell'Islam*, Centro Studi sulla Cooperazione 'A. Cammarata', S. Cataldo (Caltanissetta), 2000.

Carducci, Michele, 'La Costituzione turca al tramonto del kemalismo', *Quaderni Costituzionali*, n. 4 (2007), pp. 863–7.

Carducci, Michele and Bernardini d'Arnesano, Beatrice, *Turchia*, Il Mulino, Bologna, 2008.

Ceric, Mustafa, 'The Challenge of a single Muslim authority in Europe', *European View*, 6, 1 (December 2007).

Charnay, Jean-Paul, *Principes de stratégie arabe*, l'Herne, Paris, 2003.

Chiappero-Martinetti, Enrica, 'Dallo sviluppo economico allo sviluppo umano: quali distanze separano la Turchia dall'Unione Europea', *Il Politico*, n. 3 (2000), pp. 385–98.

Claeys, Philip and Dillen, Koen, *Turkey in the European Union. A Bridge too far*, Uit Yevenij Egmont, Brussels, 2008.

Cook, David, *Storia del Jihad. Da Maometto ai giorni nostri*, ('Understanding Jihad'), Italian translation, Einaudi, Turin, 2007.

Corrêa de Oliveira, Plinio, 'Il socialismo autogestionario rispetto al comunismo, una barriera o una tesa di ponte?', *Cristianità*, X, 82–3 (February–March 1982).

——, *Rivoluzione e Contro-Rivoluzione*, Luci sull'Est, Milan, 1998.

Cox, Caroline and Marks, John, *The West, Islam and Islamism. Is ideological Islam compatible with liberal democracy?*, Civitas, London, 2008.

Dadrian, Vahakn, *Storia del genocidio armeno. Conflitti nazionali dai Balcani al Caucaso*, Guerini e Associati, Milan, 2003.

Dalègre, Joëlle, *Grecs et Ottomans 1453–1923. De la chute de Constantinople à la disparition de l'Empire Ottoman*, L'Harmattan, Paris, 2002.

Del Valle, Alexandre, *La Turquie dans l'Europe: un cheval de Troie islamiste?*, Editions des Syrtes, Paris, 2005.

——, *Le Dilemme turc, ou les vraies raisons de la candidature d'Ankara*, Edition des Syrtes, Paris, 2006.

——, *Il totalitarismo islamista all'assalto della democrazia*, Solinum, s.l. 2007.

de Leonardis, Massimo, 'La Turchia in Europa: Turchia testa di ponte per l'Islam?', *Studi Cattolici*, n. 542, April 2006.

de Mattei, Roberto, *Guerra giusta, guerra santa. Islam e cristianesimo in guerra*, Piemme, Casale Monferrato, 2001.

——, *De Europa. Tra radici cristiane e sogni postmoderni*, Le Lettere, Florence, 2006.

——, *La dittatura del relativismo*, Solfanelli, Chieti, 2007.

de Murat, Jean, *The Great extirpation of Hellenism and Christianity in Asia Minor*, A. Triantfallis, Athens, 1999.

de Planhol, Xavier, *Les fondements géographiques de l'histoire de l'Islam*, Flammarion, Paris,1968.

de Vries, Guglielmo, SJ, *Cattolicesimo e problemi religiosi nel prossimo Oriente*, Edizioni La Civiltà Cattolica, Rome, 1944.

——, *Turchia. Situazione religiosa*, Enciclopedia Cattolica, XII (1953).

Dopfer, François, *L'imbroglio turc*, Editions Cipres de Repèns, Paris, 2008.

du Plessis, Laurent-Artur, *10 Questions sur la Turquie... et 10 réponses qui dérangent*, Jean-Cyrille Godefroy, Paris, 2005.

Eid, Camille, 'Il declino dei cristiani', *Avvenire*, 17 October 2006.

——, 'Turquie, la voie étroite des minorités', *Oasis*, n. 6 (October 2007).

Erdogan, Recep Tayyp, 'Ce que la Turquie apporte à la famille européenne', *Le Monde*, 22 October 2004.

European Commission, *2007 Regular Report Turkey*, 6 November 2007.

European Parliament, Declaration of 5 September 2006 on *The Protection and Safeguard of the Religious Heritage in the Northern Part of Cyprus.*

Faroqhi, Suraiya, *L'Impero ottomano,* Il Mulino, Bologna, 2008.

Ferguson, Neal, *XX secolo, l'età d'oro della violenza,* Itlaian translation Mondadori, Milan, 2008.

Fiorani Piacentini, Valeria (ed.), *Turchia e Mediterraneo allargato. Democrazia e Democrazie,* F. Angeli, Milan, 2006.

Flores, Marcello, *Il genocidio degli Armeni,* Il Mulino, Bologna, 2007.

Foa, Marcello, 'La Rivoluzione sotterranea', *Il Giornale,* 29 August 2007.

Freely, John, *The Western Shores of Turkey, discovering the Aegean and Mediterranean costs,* Tauris, London, 2006.

Froio, Felice, *Turchia. I Curdi. Il dramma di un popolo dimenticato,* Mursia, Milan, 1991.

Fromkin, David, *Una pace senza pace. La caduta dell'Impero ottomano,* Rizzoli, Milan, 2002.

Fuller, Graham E. Fuller and Lesser, Ian O., *Turkey's new geopolitics: from the Balkans to Western China,* Westview Press, Boulder (Colorado), 1993.

Gardet, Louis, *La Cité musulmane. Vie sociale et politique,* Vrin, Paris, 1981.

Geninazzi, Luigi, 'Non hanno risparmiato neppure l'altare di pietra . . .', *Avvenire,* 26 February 2006.

Geza, David-Pál Fodor (ed.), *Ottomans, Hungarians and Habsburgs in Central Europe. Military Confines in the Era of Ottoman Conquest,* Brill, Leiden, 2000.

Ghannouchi, Rachid, 'Le chef des islamistes tunisiens: faisons comme le Turcs!', *Courrier international,* July–August 2003.

Giscard d'Estaing, Valéry, 'Pour ou contre l'adhésion de la Turquie à l'Union européenne', intervista a *Le Monde,* 9 November 2002.

——, 'Turquie: pour le retour à la raison', *Le Figaro,* 25 November 2004.

Goffman, Daniel, *The Ottoman Empire and Early Modern*

Europe, Cambridge University Press, Cambridge 2007 (2002).

Gökalp, Ziya, *The Principles of Turkism*, translated from the Turkish and annotated by E. J. Brill, Leiden, 1968.

Goodwin, Godfrey, *The Janissaries*, Saqui, London, 2006 (1994).

Goodwin, Jason, *Lords of the Horizons. A History of the Ottoman Empire*, Vintage, London, 1998.

Greco, Vincenzo, *Greci e turchi tra convivenza e scontro. Le questioni greco-turche e la questione cipriota*, F. Angeli, Milan, 2004.

Gunter, Michael M., *The Kurds and the future of Turkey*, St Martin Press, New York, 1997.

Halecki, Oscar, *Limiti e divisioni della storia europea*, Paoline, Rome, 1962.

Harun, Arikan, *Turkey and EU*, Ashgate, Aldersot (UK), 2003.

Howe, Marvine, *Turkey. A Nation Divided over Islam's Revival*, Westview, Boulder (Colorado), 2000.

Human Rights Watch, *Violations of Free Expression in Turkey*, New York, 1999.

——, *World Report 2008. Events of 2007*, www.hrw.org

Huntington, Samuel P., *The Clash of Civilizations and the Remaking of World Order*, Touchstone Books (Simon & Schuster) New York, 1997 (first published 1996).

Impagliasso, Marco, *Una finestra sul massacro. Documenti inediti sulla strage degli armeni (1915–1916)*, Guerini e Associati, Milan, 2000.

Introvigne, Massimo, *La Turchia e l'Europa. Religione e politica nell'islam turco*, Sugarco, Milan, 2006.

Jenkins, Gareth, *Political Islam in Turkey. Running West, Heading East?*, Palgrave Macmillan, New York, 2008.

John Paul II, Pope, Speech to the Bishops' Conference of Turkey, 5 September 1994.

——, Speech to the Bishops' Conference of Turkey, 19 February 2001.

Judt, Tony, *Dopoguerra. Come è cambiata l'Europa dal 1945 a oggi*, Mondadori, Milan, 2007.

Karsch, Efraim, *Islamic Imperialism. A History*, Yale University

Press, New Haven and London, 2007.

Kaylam, Muammer, *The Kemalists. Islamic Revival and the Fate of secular Turkey*, Prometheus Books, New York, 2005.

Kinross, Patrick, *Atatürk. The Rebirth of a Nation*, Phoenix, Weidenfeld, 2001.

——, *The Ottoman Centuries. The Rise and Fall of the Turkish Empire*, Perennial, New York, 2002 (1977).

Landau, Jacob (ed.), *Atatürk and the Modernization of Turkey*, Westview Press, Boulder, 1984.

Landau, Paul, *Le Sabre et le Coran. Tariq Ramadan et les Frères Musulmans à la conquête de l'Europe*, Editions du Rocher, Paris, 2005.

Laurent, Annie, *L'Europe malade de la Turquie*, F.X. de Guibert, Paris, 2005.

Le Guillou, Gwenaelle, *L'Union Européenne et la Turquie*, Edition Apogée, Paris, 1999.

Lewis, Bernard, *La rinascita islamica*, Italian translation Il Mulino, Bologna, 1991.

——, *L'Europa e l'Islam*, ('Europe and Islam') Italian translation, Laterza, Rome-Bari, 1995.

——, *The Arabs in History*, Oxford University Press, London, 2002 (1958).

——, *The Emergency of Modern Turkey*, Oxford University Press, New York, 2002 (1961).

——, 'Europa wird am Ende des Jahrhundert islamisch sein', *Die Welt*, 28 July 2004.

Lia, Brynjar, *The Society of the Muslim Brothers in Egypt: The Rise of an Islamic Mass Movement 1928–1942*, Ithaca Press, New York, 1998.

Lorieux, Claude, *Cristiani d'Oriente nelle terre d'Islam*, Argo, Lecce, 2002.

McCarthy, Justin, *I Turchi Ottomani dalle origini al 1923*, ECIG, Genoa, 2005.

Magister, Sandro, 'Missione impossibile: costruire una Chiesa in Turchia', *L'Espresso*, 28 December 2004.

Mango, Andrew, *Turkey, the challenge of a new role*, The Center for Strategic and International Studies, Washington

DC, 1994.

——, *Atatürk. The Biography of the Founder of Modern Turkey*, Overlook Press, New York, 2002.

——, *The Turks Today*, John Murray, London, 2004 (1999).

Mansel, Philip, *Constantinople. City of World's Desire, 1453–1924*, John Murray, London, 2006 (1988).

Mantran, Robert (ed.), *Storia dell'Impero ottomano*, Argo, Lecce, 1989.

Markovich, Malka, 'Du dialogue à l'alliance des civilisations, totalitarisme de demain?', *Controverses*, n. 9 (November 2008), pp. 16–26.

Mercil, Ipek, *Les faces multiples de la modernité turque*, L'Harmattan, Paris, 2008.

Miles, I, 'Turchi e l'Europa: Italia e Turchia insieme nei Balcani', *Limes*, n. 3 (1999), pp. 183–7.

Missir de Lusignan, Livio, *Familles Latines de l'Empire Ottoman*, Les Éditions Isis, Istanbul, 2004.

Mitchell, Richard, *The Society of the Muslim Brothers*, Oxford University Press, Oxford, 1993.

Morabia, Alfred, *Le Gihad dans l'Islam médiéval*, Préface de Roger Arnaldez, Albin Michel, Paris, 1993.

Morin, Edgar, *Pensare l'Europa*, (Italian translation of 'Penser l'Europe') Garzanti, Milan. 1988.

Murawiec, Laurent, *The Mind of Jihad*, Cambridge University Press, Cambrdige, 2008.

Murray, Douglas and Verwey, Johan Pieter, *Victims of Intimidation. Freedom of Speech within Europe's Muslim Communities*, The Centre for Social Cohesion, London, 2008.

Nitoglia, Stefano, *L'Islam com'è. Un confronto con il Cristianesimo*, Preface by Gianni Baget Bozzo, Il Minotauro, Rome, 2002.

Norwich, John Julius, *Bisanzio. Splendore e decadenza di un Impero, 330–1453*, (Italian translation of 'A Short History of Byzantium') Mondadori, Milan, 2001.

O'Malley, Brendan and Craig, Ian, *The Cyprus Conspiracy, America, Espionage and the Turkish Invasion*, I. B. Tauris, London and New York, 2005.

Oddi, Silvio, 'Lettera al prof. Roberto de Mattei', *Corrispondenza Romana*, 4 August 1993.

Pacini, Andrea (ed.), *I Fratelli Musulmani e il dibattito sull'Islam politico*, Federazione Giovanni Agnelli, Turin, 1996.

Padovese, Luigi and Granella, Oriano, *Guida alla Turchia. I luoghi di san Paolo e delle origini cristiane*, Paoline, Milan, 2008.

Pamuk, Orhan, *Le voci di Istanbul: scritti e interviste*, Datanews, Rome, 2007.

Phillips, David L., 'Turkey's dream of accession', *Foreign Affairs*, n. 5 (2004).

Pera, Marcello, *Perché dobbiamo dirci cristiani. Il liberalismo, l'Europa, l'etica*, con una lettera di Benedetto XVI, Mondadori, Milan, 2008.

Pera, Marcello and Ratzinger, Joseph, *Senza radici*, Mondadori, Milan, 2004.

Pérouse, Jean-François, 'Il "mondo turco" come volontà e rappresentazione', *Limes*, n. 3 (1999), pp. 119–40.

——, *La Turquie en marche. Les grandes mutations depuis 1980*, Editions de La Martiniere, Paris, 2004.

Pin, Andrea, 'Le offese alla religione islamica. La Turchia e la Corte di Strasburgo', *Quaderni Costituzionali*, n. 1 (2006), pp. 152–4.

Pitcher, Donald Edgar, *An historical Geography of the Ottoman Empire from the earliest times to the end of the sixteenth century*, E. J. Brill, Leiden, 1972.

Pope, Hugh, *Sons of the Conquerors. The Rise of the Turkish World*, Overlook Duckworth, New York and London, 2006.

Quataert, Donalds, *The Ottoman Empire, 1700–1922*, Cambridge University Press, New York, 2007 (2000).

Ramadan, Tariq, *Il riformismo islamico. Un secolo di rinnovamento musulmano*, Città Aperta, Troina (En), 2004.

Ratzinger, Joseph, *Europa, i suoi fondamenti di oggi e domani*, San Paolo, Rome, 2004.

Razavi, Emmanuel, *Frères Musulmans dans l'ombre d'Al Qaeda*, Preface by Alexandre Del Valle, Jean-Cyrille Godefroy, Paris, 2005.

Ricci, Giovanni, *I Turchi alle porte*, Il Mulino, Bologna, 2008.

Rifkin, Jeremy, *Il sogno europeo. Come l'Europa ha creato una nuova visione del futuro che sta lentamente eclissando il sogno americano*, (Italian translation of 'The European Dream, How Europe's Vision of the Future is Quietly Eclipsing the American Dream') (New York, Penguin, 2004), Mondadori, Milan, 2004.

Rosselli, Alberto, *Sulla Turchia e l'Europa*, Solfanelli, Chieti, 2006.

——, *L'olocausto armeno. Breve storia di un massacro dimenticato*, Solfanelli, Chieti, 2007.

Roy, Olivier, *Généalogie de l'Islamisme*, Hachette, Paris, 1995.

——, *La Turquie aujourd'hui: un pays européen?*, Ed. Universalis, Paris, 2004.

Rubin, Michael, 'Con Erdogan la Turchia rischia una rivoluzione islamica', *L'Occidentale*, 23 April 2008.

Sale, Giovanni, *Stati islamici e minoranze cristiane*, Jaca Books, Milan, 2008.

Santoro, Andrea, *Lettere dalla Turchia*, Città Nuova, Rome, 2007.

Schaller, Dominik J. and Zimmerer, Jürgen, *Late Ottoman Genocides. The dissolution of the Ottoman Empire and Young Turkish Population and Extermination Policies*, Routledge, London, 2009.

Schulze, Reinhard, *Il mondo islamico nel XX secolo. Politica e società civile (1994)*, Feltrinelli, Milan, 2004.

Sécher, Reynald, *La Vendée-vengée: le génocide franco-français*, Presses Universitares de France, Paris, 1986.

Sharon, Rachel and Krespin, Rachel, 'Fethullah Gülens Grand Ambition', *The Middle East Quarterly* (winter 2009), pp. 55–66.

Shäuble, Wolfang and Phillips, David L., 'Talking Turkey', *Foreign Affairs*, n. 6 (2004).

Solomon, Som and Alamaqdisi, Elyias, *The Mosque exposed*, ANM Press, Charlottesville (Virginia), 2007.

Sookhdeo, Patrick, *Global Jihad. The Future in the Face of Militant Islam*, Isaac Publishing, McLean (VA), 2007.

Spencer, Robert (ed.), *The Myth of Islamic Tolerance. How Islamic Law treats Non-Muslims*, Prometheus Book, New York, 2003.

Spinelli, Barbara, 'La Turchia e l'Europa. La nuova potenza Eurasia', *La Stampa*, 19 December 2004.

Stürminger, Walter (ed.), *Die Türken von Wien in Augenzeugenberichten*, Munich, 1983.

Summer, Chris, *The Rise and Fall of a Drug Empire*, BBC News, 7 April 2006.

Tazaghart, Armand and Jacquard, Roland, 'Les légions européennes du Jihad', *Le Figaro Magazine*, 16 July 2005.

Tega, Diletta, 'La laicità turca alla prova di Strasburgo', *Diritto Pubblico e comparato europeo*, I (2005).

Tendler, Stewart, 'Drug Godfather's reign of Terror ends', *The Times*, 1 February 2006.

Ternon, Yves, *Lo Stato criminale. I genocidi del XX secolo*, Corbaccio, Milan, 1997.

——, *Gli armeni. 1915–1916: il genocidio dimenticato*, Preface by Antonia Arslan, Rizzoli, Milan, 2007.

Tibi, Bassam, *Il fondamentalismo religioso*, Bollati Boringhieri, Turin, 1997.

——, *Euro-Islam. L'integrazione mancata*, Marsilio, Venice, 2003.

——, 'Europeanizing Islam, or the Islamization of Europe', Timothy, Byrnes and Peter, Katzenstein (eds), *Religion in an Expanding Europe*, Cambridge University Press, New York, 2006.

——, *Con il velo in Europa? La grande sfida della Turchia*, Salerno, Rome, 2008.

——, 'Islamists Approach Europe', *The Middle East Quarterly*, winter 2009, pp. 47–54.

Toynbee, Arnold, *The Western Question in Greece and Turkey. A Study in the Contact of Civilization*, H. Fertig, New York, 1970.

Trifkovic, Serge, *Islam. History, Theology, Impact in the World*, Regina Orthodox Press, Boston, 2002.

Ugur, Mehmet Canefe Nergis, *Turkey and European integration: accession, prospects and issues*, Routledge,

London and New York, 2004.

Utkan, Nekati, 'La Turchia e l'Europa', *Rivista di studi politici internazionali*, n. 2 (2003).

Vahide, Sükran, *Islam in Modern Turkey. An Intellectual Biography of Bedinzzaman Said Nursi*, State University of New York Press, Albany (New York), 2005.

Van Aalderen, Maarten, 'L'eredità di Atatürk e il velo islamico', *Aspenia*, n. 42 (2008).

Verez, Jean Claude and Chaponnière, Jean Raphaël, *Turquie et Union Européenne: un défi réciproque*, Ellipse, Paris, 2005.

Verluise, Pierre, *Fondamentaux de l'Union européenne. Démographie, économie, géopolitique*, Ellipses, Paris, 2008.

Vidino, Lorenzo, 'Aims and Methods of Europe's Muslim Brotherhood', *Current Trends in Islamist Ideology*, n. 4 (2006), pp. 22–44.

Vielmini, Fabrizio, 'Dal Turan all'Eurasia', *Limes*, n. 3 (1999), pp. 151–62.

Vignelli, Guido, 'L'immigrazionismo: un progetto di tribalizzazione dell'Europa?', Carosa, Alberto and Vignelli, Guido, *L'invasione silenziosa. L'immigrazione: risorsa o complotto?*, Il Minotauro, Rome, 2002.

Weiler, Joseph, *Un'Europa Cristiana. Un saggio esplorativo*, BUR, Milan, 2003.

White, Jenny B., *Islamist Mobilization in Turkey. A Study in Vernacular Politics*, University of Washington Press, Seattle (Wa), 2002.

Yavuz, M. Hakan, *Islam Political Identity in Turkey*, Oxford University Press, Oxford and New York, 2003.

Zarcone, Thierry, *Secret et sociétés secretes en Islam: Turquie, Iran et Asie centrale, XIX–XXème siècles. Franc-Masonerie, Carboneria et Confréries sonfies*, Arché, Milan, 2002.

——, *La Turquie moderne et l'Islam*, Flammarion, Paris, 2004.

——, *La Turquie. De l'Empire Ottoman à la République d'Atatürk*, Gallimard, Paris, 2005.

Zürcher, Erik J., *Storia della Turchia dalla fine dell'Impero ottomano ai giorni nostri*, Donzelli, Roma, 2007.